COLLECTED POEMS
1930-1960

By the Same Author

A BRAVERY OF EARTH

READING THE SPIRIT

SONG AND IDEA

POEMS, NEW AND SELECTED

BURR OAKS

SELECTED POEMS

UNDERCLIFF

GREAT PRAISES

★

With Selden Rodman

WAR AND THE POET
An Anthology

COLLECTED POEMS
1930-1960

——— ❋ ———

Richard Eberhart

INCLUDING
51 NEW POEMS

NEW YORK
OXFORD UNIVERSITY PRESS
1960

FIRST PUBLISHED 1960

Third printing, 1969

To

BETTY

RICK and GRETCHEN

Acknowledgments

SOME of the new poems in this book were first published in the following publications, to whose Editors I am grateful for permission to reprint them here.

The American Scholar, Art News, Audience, The Beloit Poetry Journal, Botteghe Oscure, Contemporary Poetry, The Colorado Review, Experiment, The Grecourt Review, The Hudson Review, Inventario, The Kenyon Review, The Ladies' Home Journal, The London Magazine, The London Times Literary Supplement, Mandrake, Mutiny, The Nation, The New Yorker, The New Republic, Northern Review, Poetry London – New York, Poetry – A Magazine of Verse, Poetry New York, Poetry Northwest, Platform, The Prairie Schooner, Spectrum, The Transatlantic Review, Trinity Review, The Virginia Quarterly Review, Voices, Wake.

Contents

From A BRAVERY OF EARTH

From READING THE SPIRIT

From SONG AND IDEA

Contents

From BURR OAKS

Contents

From POEMS, NEW AND SELECTED

From SELECTED POEMS

From UNDERCLIFF

Contents

From GREAT PRAISES

Contents

NEW POEMS

Contents

THIS FEVERS ME

This fevers me, this sun on green,
On grass glowing, this young spring.
The secret hallowing is come,
Regenerate sudden incarnation,
Mystery made visible
In growth, yet subtly veiled in all,
Ununderstandable in grass,
In flowers, and in the human heart,
This lyric mortal loveliness,
The earth breathing, and the sun.
The young lambs sport, none udderless.
Rabbits dash beneath the brush.
Crocuses have come; wind flowers
Tremble against quick April.
Violets put on the night's blue,
Primroses wear the pale dawn,
The gold daffodils have stolen
From the sun. New grass leaps up;
Gorse yellows, starred with day;
The willow is a graceful dancer
Poised; the poplar poises too.
The apple takes the seafoam's light,
And the evergreen tree is densely bright.
April, April, when will he
Be gaunt, be old, who is so young?
This fevers me, this sun on green,
On grass glowing, this young spring.

O WILD CHAOS!

O wild Chaos! O sweet Chaos!
Dance to my arms, I would lie with you,
With your last dancing garment off!
O sweet Chaos! O wild Chaos!

I

Let me get you in hilarious weight
With the maddest world's merriest child.
Sweet, sweet Chaos with burningest lips,
And your limbs, they make a goddess unable!
Come to me with your giddiest love,
Wild, wild, sweet, sweet Chaos!

THE BELLS OF A CHINESE TEMPLE

The bells of a Chinese temple sang
A monody in sunned Sabang,
A singing timbreless of tone,
Like water falling on a stone.
And he was glad, glad to be
A sailor resting from the sea
Where Indians and Arabs go,
Most slowly, slow and slow;
Where swart Malayan women walk
Dreamfully along and talk;
Where skirted, bearded, dark-skin Turks
Go hand in hand, and no one works.
China women with bound doll feet
Like marionettes move down the street,
And underneath the arbored trees,
Mild-eyed, squatting in twos or threes,
Chinamen smoke, peaceful and still,
Gazing afar at the palms on the hill,
Pondering Buddha, these Chinamen—
Or counting their hoarded yen.
And there are girls whose smiles are worth
Some subtle Asiatic mirth
Understood and wonderful:
Girls dark, and shy, and beautiful.

He had not known harbor or town
So free from tumult, fret, or frown,

2

Of all the sunny towns that are
Spun under a southern star
Upon the Oriental South.
Here Love with amorous mellow mouth
Drinks from the chalice of delight
Sun-mulled wine from dawn till night.
Here the ponderer plucks a lute;
The drowsed land is ripe with fruit;
And all man's conquest and man's glory
Is but a story-teller's story,
Incredible and strangely told
Of men far off amazed with gold,
Who bend beneath some heavy plan
To trample down a fellow-man,
Thus harvest wealth, and fame, and power.

This is Sebang; hour on hour
The full day ripens in the sun,
And time has always just begun.
Primeval silence without stir
Holds the earth like gossamer;
For love is slowly blossoming
In quietness too still to sing,
From which all passions green or ripe
Are shadowy blooms of the Immortal Type.

And here he lingers, murmuring
The name of some forgotten king,
Who had a wonder-welling heart:
Richard Ghormley Eberhart.

MAZE

I have a tree in my arm,
There are two hounds in my feet,
The earth can do me no harm
And the lake of my eyes is sweet.

But a fire has burnt the tree down,
I have no blood for the hounds.
Why has the will made me a crown
For a human mind that has bounds?

Who made the tree? Who made fire?
The hounds have gone back to the master.
The earth has killed my desire
That leaped up faster and faster.

It is man did it, man,
Who imagined imagination,
And he did what man can,
He uncreated creation.

There is no tree in my arm,
I have no hounds in my feet,
The earth can soothe me and harm,
And the lake of my eyes is a cheat.

FOR A LAMB

I saw on the slant hill a putrid lamb,
Propped with daisies. The sleep looked deep,
The face nudged in the green pillow
But the guts were out for crows to eat.

Where's the lamb? whose tender plaint
Said all for the mute breezes.
Say he's in the wind somewhere,
Say, there's a lamb in the daisies.

CARAVAN OF SILENCE

(For J. L. Sweeney)

Third with silence in a tent
He, unamazed in meditation,
Looked up from Persia, where he sent
Spiraling wings beyond Creation.

Drowsily the one beside him
Laid his elbow on sleep,
Wines of sunned hills denied him
Moods of moods he could not keep;
He slept, with night living around
Like sea on a dark-fathomed plant.
His was a silence without sound
To beetle, grasshopper, or ant.
Camels and he like dunes would sleep
Till the gold ball came over,
Then stray the tedious journey, keep
The mild destiny of the rover:
Hunger and sleep, and the slight
Untroubling dreams, ununderstood,
And never labouring the farsight
Of cities where no cities stood.

Drowsily he breathed. But by him,
Posed, the second sat, gave out
Upon the vast of thoughts that sky him
Silence to make the stars shout.
The audible bloom of night
He heard bell and rebell desire;
His silence trembled the world, that might
Give back and echo and inspire.
He toed warm sand, probed
His fingers through the warm air.
Purpose by the night was robed
Secure. He fought no despair.

5

There is a green land, and water
Clear as the night is scarved, place
Where wait wife and daughter,
And the opal, unborn face.
The wish is a loud silence
And the hope is a star power
That shake night with innocence
Soft hour on dark hour.
Thus he, the second silence, flung
A bold tone he could recapture.
The cloth of night about him hung,
He took the stigmata of rapture.

But a ghost form was the third
Man, and his stillness stiller
Than song of an unborn bird.
Night chilled, and grew chiller.
The tent was not need for him;
Nor destiny. Not a star
Walked, a smooth-limbed god and slim,
But things were what they are.
Less than stillness, silence
He winged beyond Creation, he
Full with indifference,
And head bent near to his knee.
Lips murmured a thought's births;
And curled, and eased. The oldness
Of sun and man he knew, earth's
Coldness and goldenness.
Night aged and pearled
To a dawn; yet the philosopher
Turned the globed world
Colder and goldener.

FOUR LAKES' DAYS

I

Summery Windermere, sweet lake!
Where eyes wake wide to see again
And the fields, O clover earth-breath take
On the roads, in the warmed-away rain;
Then Far, and then Near Sawrey
Are; foot-increasing Esthwaite
Water is, O the green! far, see
What you will, walk. There's a late
Spell on the hills, will break not,
A gentlest mystery like a fate,
Something serene, you cannot take not
On Hawkshead Hills. Blare on the air,
Bagpipes! 'tis the merry-hearted note—
Thus you change, hill and valley share,
Feel each, know none by rote.

Young ferns by time-retaining tarn
Lose something of goldenness: height
Down-dooms, moves along the tarn;
(In poised fragility, my fright)
My heart leapt down, so with gloom
Leaded and time-encased, I shied
From the tremor, the small room
Of (bleak tarn!) all that has died.
Glen Mary unsilences; slight
Whispery waterfall, then such
Tossing laughter as can fight
Rocks, and overcome them much.
On heart-beat and feet go, he, I,
Who than happiness happier be
Keeping earth joined to the sky,
Locking, in love, earth and the sea.

But, topped, stop. Somehow
Miser it, lest the mind

7

Race beyond the senses' pace
And the whole being nothing find.
Valley-volleying blackbird (how new)
Another flier has; sheep can
With a strange passion bleat; there grew
In spider's earth-sight something of man.

In air-shiver against white wall
A flower, blue, incandescent
Does dance on the eye-ball;
It makes beauty effervescent.
At Fell Foot (charm) farm. Rob
This, clover-over-the-dales;
Smells of cows; good hob-
Nail, spike my ear! and kissing pails.

Till the twilight folds and all's
As blue as the bluewashed walls.

II

Point-pushed by the wind, rain
With penetrating excellency
Scrawls all the hills, writes plain
Its unread-yet charactery.
Now in wet morning be, begin,
Wrynose Pass to Cockley Beck,
Ramp, suck the thick damps in,
From cheek no lightest rain-flake fleck,
But all is watery world-of-love.
Up (darkly, slowly) Hard Knott Pass
To the bleak. There, mind's of
Not the tenderness of the grass.

So lean the weather-fabricked eye
And build the chilly-mossy dell
From universal motleyed sky
To this ten feet of world, of fell.

Not the woundedness of the soul;
Of desire, the joy. And, soaked all day,
Sky, earth make each other whole,
You between, cold mote in the gray.
Leave Duddon for Woolpack Inn.
'The way's by the little stone men
Over the moor.' She said, whose thin
Skin at the cheeks thought youth again;
'Turn left by yon leafy tree.'
Her winter she turned to the valley.
So he, I go, we
Slow to the pelt-rain-drum's rally-
Of-loneliness in rained-on weather.
Fluffed, but damp, and moving, boulders
Bleat, all hill-huddled together.
Hump up their pointed shoulders
The little men, fearful, who dare not
The Druid haunt; but they can lead
By bitter Burnmoor tarn! and care not
For anything but the earth-need.

The low skies lip the lost lake,
I quiver to taste the dead sight,
But to my lips the colour, livid, take—
Sca Fell scales his hoar height!
And I make to the bleak Screes
Where the rain is alive, though dark,
Thread through wild rain on my knees,
To Wast Water. The misty mark

Calls. And I sleep to hear
The fine, moist lungs of atmosphere.

III

Labour them, these drenched heights.
Put foot to dusky sky-dropped pearls

That rope the grass with their frail lights,
Spring from the shelly strength, it hurls
You up! and at Windy Gap
A born cloud will take you, lake you
Around in its fresh frothy sap;
And the pulsation will shake you.
Speedy steady wind-of-mist
Blew up the side, the ledge combed it;
Stream out the fledgling and me-kissed
Spumy streamers and I roamed it,
Happy-shawled, the high valley air
In the condensing and tight cloak,
My new body-skin and fay's hair;
And clean, and wet, and warm soak.
See it cling its youth together
Slowly over the valley rolling,
Fluffing a myriad down-feather,
Coyly downward. Whole-bring
Your ghosts here; and all-take
The gleams here, sense, sense,
Through the sun's eye of this lake;
Till Black Sail's sound of waterfall
Tries; and you are down the hill.

The Northern man, with a ripe lung,
Found vagabond, can fill
A dale with his nutty tongue.

Climb up Scarth Gap, lit
Dismally by foreboding clouds,
And at the top, the desolate pit
Portends with dull baleful shrouds;
Must wear the rock, bound solitude
Like a leaden, and forlorn hope,
Or like a worn, lost brood
Of these, that crowd and grope,
Stumble, fumble, mell down

Into the sun-on-the-hill sheer
Prospect sweet and, there, town,
The final soft of Buttermere.

Lie on stone bridge and be lulled
A long time in the gold shocks
Of trembling stream; till all's dulled
But the sombre shine of under rocks.

That light will deepen and well, in
Snug sleep, under Helvellyn.

IV

Contend with steepness, the dark air
Unshapes the mountain as it grows
More misty-moody. Pace it bare
Up into the stormy throes,
A certain waft of rotting fern
Gone by in the severe, clean
Feel of wild electric burn,
Needles of ice-like rain in the sheen
Of darkening lambency and surrounding
Tempest, as the clashing sound-of- ,
Clamour clouds, mountain-bounding
Grow to a groan through the pound of
Immense winds in the gloom-nude space.
Lost, and aware, with hard, clear
Climb, steer at the force in your face
Through the tightening, soft, obscure
Orbit of dark inhospitality,
And the powerful blood dominant leaps
Up at the dreadful world-majesty,
At the bleak raging energy it keeps
Stupendous tempo striking the rock
With slant steel feet, with mailed flesh
Commands the creep-on fog, block, block

With blackest waste its trembling, fresh,
Impetuous urge. At the felt top
The violent wind and rain shake
Exultation, and time ceases,
The pulses jangle as if to break,
The churning chaos choas increases,
A surge of demonic energy unites
Blood and the bitter world-vitality
As the flaying and flayed being ignites
In elemental passion intensity
Satanic, angelic, one harmony
Of immense glory like fire clinging
A blaze of terrible immediacy
The wild blood of freedom singing
Descending the clanging cliff rungs
By its own impulse hurled,
Shouting with soundless, taut lungs
Into the powerful, dark world,
Catharsis of the soul triumphant
Through suffering and effort, death
Purged from the bones militant,
The gift of God, pure mortal breath.

There's tremble in all solitude,
Be at, in this: it's in you, times.
Nothing of evil or of good,
But the quiverness, sometimes.
It is given. Yet, feel-less
How often, we, fallen fell adown
From our free skyey realness,
Too close to men-mesh and town.

Mystery is for ever the same.
Wake into the life of flame.

ODE TO SILENCE

Be Silence from your dismal cave abroad,
Nor moist rocks sweet with rain, nor mosses
Lately drenched, that swell the broken sky,
Postpone, now mellow doors of fragrant air,
Your stealthy moving cloak here where we die.
Come from your grot, the last power left to laud.
For she lies dead, and agony can no more.
Sun light on ebon hair. Be one witness,
Though strange noon, with hurtful whisper-shine
Crowds down the sky, on golden chords that tear.
With surety firm and deep as ocean's roar,
From dauntless throat, that moans and wails all year,
Be hourly spreading tenderness no tongue
Can call, O steadfast force in sojourn here,
From region dim of love, but something young.
So shall we join, so both pour out our store,
By tarns of melancholy heights of hills,
Or on torn cringeing sands of deserts, there,
Or barren knolls, abrupt from wide valleys clear,
Or wandering among the tribes of snow.
How have I kept the eagle eye for you!
Discoverer ever haunted with new worlds.
Consent to me, and dare to seem
The fervent armour of my skin.
Thus quell the risen anguish rude.
Stillness, be my plight: mate with song.
Then action's fortunes must, as avid wires
Reverberate, be vocal calm.
When the bumble-bee drew down the clover nod,
But gentle, shook the dozing afternoon
With his dry burn, and all the royal compeers
Helped moan the cooling earth to your full boon,
O Shadow born! then was an end of tears.
Orchard's grass, and the Septembered sod
Slumbered, and covered over were green fears.

No foam stirs forth from out the milkweed pod.
No bird can step, but earth's whole nature hears
Its little spring, and pleasured, seems to croon.
O joyless land, of wilderness
Increasing strong, dread solitude,
And now the sky brazen and stiff.
Why must all ways be closed
Against me miserable
From the fount of joy
And springs of innocence,
I left in this harsh world alive.
We die with her as all close with their dead.
Now walks full midnight, O make no moan for her,
Now bind time's mantle, the dark cloth, in folds
Around, to spirit same as fleshly stir;
That the mutual control a hoped life hold
In shroud, the flowered interment of the years.
Whence comes some nameless peace that still enfolds,
Though the world sadden, and new pain has bled
Ere the old is stilled. With Silence, in dank wolds,
Or humid meres, mostly worship her.
Ah, wounded more, in earth's increasing ways,
Be sound the kind counterpart of need.
Hear the grieving Chinese gongs emball
Woe's Aeon, and roll it in a hollow note
On the world. And now the softer drone
Of the love-lute in Sumatra, yet remote.
There, against Girgenti's temples thrown,
Some careless boys for Pan pipe simple lays,
And sing Sicilian airs, too fleetly flown.
Slow flows the moist Alpine horn, and falls
Mournful from the mountain's lucid stone,
The perfect lament, and threne of sorrow's throat.
All sound is ladened! when human means
Reach forth. Then listen the earth sings
Faithful to itself, unknown.
Clairvoyant, be as a cool sea shell,

Constrained, with hurtless ear
Whirled on the gentle roar,
To the impersonal impersonal
That delicate ravishments in the mind come.
Yet plainly I hear our unyielding voices cry
In the long suffering that knows no close,
Nor earth smothers, to rise on lark note through,
Or like the crickets sing. Aye, even our woes
Recumbent, seem to fever forth with clue
Of other sorrw, and our instruments sigh
To wean us from that deeper natal rue.
Soft mineral, instruct the bell to die;
Fibres, be wood of waxen-sculpted stop;
Dry thong be lyric, in catgut's chilled throes.
Earth sees her no longer, no more her beauty
Lingers. Love lights us no more. No longer
Love overcomes us, and maims us, and will kill.
Be earth of strength to make us the stronger.
Be this the will, we selfed, enriched in her will.
To move, through this midnight, somewhat free,
Under the sumptuous warping cloak, until,
As sap can yearn though Destiny stand a tree,
We wander, but will kiss the white star light,
O sovereign lovely Silence accept, be me.
Your kingdom's in the wayward wind
In waft of ease above March bulbs,
Where too you pulse.
The sea-mew finds you after his call.
The dusk ferns
Are yours, when the sun's bceome their own;
And a green shine they lend to the small brook;
Then thronging minnows, like lights, are seen to play.
O joyful land, of solitude
Brimming bright, loved rarity,
And the heart outgrows passion and pain.
Vibrance is on the violet now.
See, the whole sky trembles, mirroring

One simple flower. Stillness quivers, and forces
Vision inward from the eye.
There is one way, to creep up the purple tunnel
And draw on that tender canopy;
Thence from happy shadowy
Contentment, look outward
Secure, with world bright immaculate eye.
Quivery are in all earth and ocean Silences,
Whether fire's or ice's, or loams' or stones'.
By smallest ellwand touch the deep moonglade
Until our harmless obsequies are done.
Firstly luminous in the beginning,
All things sing Silence to the perfect sun.
Flowing starlight, like a frozen thing,
And mountain, like a fusion not yet made,
The rayless mind relume, and in it ring
(By gyres on gyres of harmonies quickening)
In changeless radiancy that casts no shade:
Universal fire mothers its piping light.

THE RETURN OF ODYSSEUS

My disappointments, large as capsized tugs,
Pull no more the big ship of love.
My eye of fire, motionable coal,
That saw such salutations of the wharf
(And piped a hoot to the woman's tooting colours)
Is out, and weeps annual delugings;
My engines bucked and wrung. My
Timbers' splinters plaything water patterns,
My sturdy and few tons have gone to roost
Under the infant waters of the sea,
That never grew to man's curious abyss,
Nor walked a brain in the aching shape of dream
Along the narrow deck of singing timber:
What a boisterous business, to be a guide.
But in the nest of nature's slippery scope,

(Where of God the pressure is so tight)
Elongate eyes like spears would be
Would spasm the cranky juice of hatred's darlings,
Spend the volatile dyes of woman's dress,
Precursor of the sorrow's end. Unheard
The cock in the waters crows, Good Night,
There is nothing to do but be swayed by the sea.

While with gynæcologistic hands
My hempen fingers purged, I had eased
To birth my iron monstrous love.

'WHERE ARE THOSE HIGH AND HAUNTING SKIES'

Where are those high and haunting skies,
Higher than the see-through wind? Where are
The rocky springs beyond desire? And where
The sudden source of purity?

Now they are gone again. Though world
Decrease the wraith-like eye so holy,
And bring a summer in, and with it folly,
Though the senses bless and quell,

I would not with such blessings be beguiled.
But seek an image far more dear. Oh where
Has gone that madness wild? Where stays
The abrupt essence and the final shield?

SUITE IN PRISON

I

The grave's a seed will get some monstrous bloom
To drowse the mind with warm eternity
And nourish the stupor on unending time
Until dull numbness gluts the feeling power,
Then close its final grandeur down and dark
The last clear beams of bright mortality.

The skeletons of lovers, let them then
Rejoice since no hot hurried consummation
Vagues their joy or surfeits fond desire;
The earth is long at marrying the bone.
Let fleshless jaws make smile at butterflies
And humour have and jest at humming birds
Since these have got their moment wooing done
Before the axle of the earth has turned,
Or harvested a wormy crop of moons;
But they sink deeper in abysmal love
And in the slowest satisfying lust
Are tightened, till they get great regiments
Of babes with petal spears to pierce the air.

Bull worms will probe my sockets, move among
The loosening channels of my brain for food,
But how, when they recoil from some hard tissue
Bitter to their taste, shall they surmise
Stout Plato with his knotted dream of God,
How guess the Christ-idea marbled there?
And when the brain's last particle is worm
How shall the worms high triumph celebrate
And how rejoice for hugy victory?

II

That which is at your East, your heart, I cannot
Tell how it shapes with mine, thus to admit
By a fine dexterity our equal pleasures.
It is too bad we do not in Universals sit.
You have your South, I mine, joyful, painful,
To which each goes; and gets from, fangs' stings.
But we must burn there, that some fire stay
Which nested the thick Phoenix-matrix of things.
It seems the West is to us both plainest;
Escapeless; stopless and blackest. We are so
Blights in the tall scent of this crouching hunger.
To devour the race. Thus let another grow.
Hearts, testicles and gall, we defeat
At the head, our Winter; with eyes' changeless white
Got gazing in that mirror, supernal earth.
And there, whirl, chilly, swift, and replete.
Yet in all this intercommunion I feel with you,
I weep the foreign waste of your close brow.
Leave me. Alone I can pluck up a looking-glass,
And say my own eyes to my own eyes are, now.

III

I turned where the sun came up and he held my hand,
The fair lily of lingering in his hand.
Where he walked, freshening over the land
He plucked me up from the fragrant land.
His breast was smooth and smelt like pleasure,
Joyfully I bent and kissed my treasure.
His skin rippled senstitive as fingers;
Peacefully I touched together my fingers.
I lay on the green earth moist as grass
And I reached, but the sky was not grass,
O weep alone! I wept on the world,

And weeping came back over the waste world.
I turned face down to the mean loam,
The worms all choired come home.
Than a flame lit in my thighs and feet;
I ran away, yet not feeling my feet.

I turned where the sun went down the dark,
And a hand was on me, hairy and dark!
As he rushed, looming out from the earth
He tore me up from the fervent earth.
And a monstrous wailing destroyed the air.
But no one was there; no one in the air.
Screaming, faint, I peered down to the ground
Praying for the womb of the black ground.

IV

Incarcerating sunlight, world damnation,
Now am I crisped in the great blight of all.
Incantation of might, my personal laudation,
To you, now, at last, from me must befall.
Power blest, against blasphemy Hate
Lies down a spent child with not one sigh.
Beyond hope, we are destroyed to create
Anew, paeons in the killing sky.
I cannot combust off the skin-grown sun.
Darkness proffers no help and cold no chill.
Pitiful in incandescence, Furies of action
Dancing, their impotent conquests distil.
Angels of solitude, immured in monuments
Of cruel hours, malignant despairs instil.
Vision without memory has no portents.
Future, terrible and evil, be me, I will.

V

THE BATH ROOM

Shoes, table, light, and telephone.
The polished hides point to the wall.
They want their grass. And some antique cow
Likes the mild wash of the pagoda bells.
And I'll on no pillow moan,
Nor in the balefires fight,
But call up the Wolf, and hear him rasp,
And say I'm in this room tonight.
Some other storm, come cut the wires down!

Those kissing hides. This glass-refracted light;
Whose incestuous brother fails his love to tell;
And if it were possible, I'd swing on a willow.

Khubla, but with mailed boots. Akhnaton
With a taper. The Beast ravens, without our change.
I stand bolt upright, reading the paper.

The table wears its faultless, white surplice.
Fixes, waiting for an elbow.
Shall I dart down my diamond eye
And all its fibres try to tear?

No, I shall stand in the middle of this room
And not note the soles of my feet.
Not front the swords of the light.
Not brave the yells of the Wolf.
Not be adamant-minded in the middle
Of this doom. But with sweet acclaim
(By the bedside) modulate the name
(Light, shoes, and telephone),
Of the albino crow, of the table.

VI

Lord, stabilise me. My legs
Fail in the white crevasses. My hands
To thin husks are twisted. My bones
In the high winds can stand no more.

Blood, that built the heavy world,
Curls in the shells it built,
Thins and congeals. Its cold heart
Would turn to the earth, its home.

Eyes, the last levellers of the world,
Have lost direction and show false,
The rare air them avails
With many ways of ice and snow.

Of glassy temples crinkling white
Glittering all the icy air,
As cold a city and as bright
As flicks in the tight air of a child.

Lord, stabilise me. My pride
Walks with inebriate legs. My desire
Eats up the whole world. My love
In its big excess destroys me.

Lord, qualify me. To see
Pride floored like a marionette;
Desire fulfilled like a marriage;
And love of sweet use in the world.

Lord, admit me. To rejoice
Even within the abysm of suffering.
Contain me in Thine atmosphere, Lord.
And in the dancing of Thine ecstasy.

THE GROUNDHOG

In June, amid the golden fields,
I saw a groundhog lying dead.
Dead lay he; my senses shook,
And mind outshot our naked frailty.
There lowly in the vigorous summer
His form began its senseless change,
And made my senses waver dim
Seeing nature ferocious in him.
Inspecting close his maggots' might
And seething cauldron of his being,
Half with loathing, half with a strange love,
I poked him with an angry stick.
The fever arose, became a flame
And Vigour circumscribed the skies,
Immense energy in the sun,
And through my frame a sunless trembling.
My stick had done nor good nor harm.
Then stood I silent in the day
Watching the object, as before;
And kept my reverence for knowledge
Trying for control, to be still,
To quell the passion of the blood;
Until I had bent down on my knees
Praying for joy in the sight of decay.
And so I left; and I returned
In Autumn strict of eye, to see
The sap gone out of the groundhog,
But the bony sodden hulk remained.
But the year had lost its meaning,
And in intellectual chains
I lost both love and loathing,
Mured up in the wall of wisdom.
Another summer took the fields again
Massive and burning, full of life,
But when I chanced upon the spot

There was only a little hair left,
And bones bleaching in the sunlight
Beautiful as architecture;
I watched them like a geometer,
And cut a walking stick from a birch.
It has been three years, now.
There is no sign of the groundhog.
I stood there in the whirling summer,
My hand capped a withered heart,
And thought of China and of Greece,
Of Alexander in his tent;
Of Montaigne in his tower,
Of Saint Theresa in her wild lament.

THE RAPE OF THE CATARACT

King Prajadhipok his cataract
Doctor Samson held within his hand
Walking down an aisle of attendant
Princes, and maids, awaiting the outcome.

There, of obscured Oriental vision
Was an end, and caul; breathlessly
The ten Private Secretaries, the General,
The Admiral, the established flunkies

Saw the veil drawn off the ancient East,
Rejoiced at Oriental Americanisation,
Made delicate bows, appropriate sighs;
While below the Court clicked billiard balls.

The Royal surgery (decor by Le Corbusier),
As palace made into an hospital
Reeked not at all of the lotus blossom,
Nor of perfumed cigars, but stank

Very slightly of an overt efficiency,
The time element increasing anxiety
To see, or not to see, if to be seen
(From Bangkok to New York) the western world

While the dapper Minister in excelsis
Haunting each crevice of the vast palace
With feline graces, a misplaced Machiavelli,
Sipped his calculated Eastern tea

Having a score or more of gentle daggers
Concealed in his innate gentility
But not a fleck or flash of any eyelash
Took aim and stock of failure, of success;

Djin comes in. His Excellency whines.
And then my suave and gentle Chirasakti,
Adopting a smile, is waited upon
By Smaksman like a bird with bugle eyes.

Now hail the light! His Majesty appears
As the neat procession of success begins
Flanked by attendants in a soft fatigue
As the King's hayfever shakes a silken handkerchief.

The President of the United States must wait,
And while his jaws contract, His Majesty
Upon the lush parterre with Djin and Ajja
Makes timid, deft essays with a model airplane

Its little rubber bands expanding
As with a gentle whirr it takes the air
To soar ten feet, then, glory-spent, it dashes
At the feet of the King's frightened Secretary.

And now the Royal Party moves in state
To the mansion's chief balcony; there arrayed

It views the proper burst and display of fireworks'
Perfunctive poppings on the feckless earth below

For Western vision now succeeds the Eastern,
Radios, picture palaces, and television
Make a regal triumph at the Royal Court,
And Their Majesties retire, amused and pleased

To see the President, and shake his hand
For fresh experiences in the West all eager
And then departing in a bolt of motors
They seek the City, while still Buddha smiles.

1934

Caught upon a thousand thorns, I sing,
Like a rag in the wind,
Caught in the blares of the automobile horns
And on the falling airplane's wing.
Caught napping in my study
Among a thousand books of poetry.

Doing the same thing over and over again
Brings about an obliteration of pain.
Each day dies in a paper litter
As the heart becomes less like a rapier.
In complexity, feeling myself absurd
Dictating an arbitrary word,

My self my own worst enemy,
Hunting the past through all its fears,
That on the brain that glory burst
Bombing a ragged future's story,
Caught in iron individuality
As in the backwash of a sea

Knowing not whether to fight out,
Or keep silent; to talk about the weather,

Or rage again through wrong and right,
Knowing knowledge is a norm of nothing,
And I have been to the Eastern seas
And walked on all the Hebrides.

Ashamed of loving a long-practised selfhood,
Lost in a luxury of speculation,
At the straight grain of a pipe I stare
And spit upon all worlds of Spain;
Time like a certain sedative
Quelling the growth of the purpose tree.

Aware of the futility of action,
Of the futility of prayer aware,
Trying to pry from the vest of poetry
The golden heart of mankind's deep despair,
Unworthy of a simple love
In august, elected worlds to move

Stern, pliant in the modern world, I sing,
Afraid of nothing and afraid of everything,
Curtailing joy, withholding irony,
Pleased to condemn contemporaneity
Seeking the reality, skirting
The dangerous absolutes of fear and hope,

And I have eased reality and fiction
Into a kind of intellectual fruition
Strength in solitude, life in death,
Compassion by suffering, love in strife,
And ever and still the weight of mystery
Arrows a way between my words and me.

In a hard intellectual light
I will kill all delight,
And I will build a citadel
Too beautiful to tell

O too austere to tell
And far too beautiful to see,
Whose evident distance
I will call the best of me.

And this light of intellect
Will shine on all my desires,
It will my flesh protect
And flare my bold constant fires,

For the hard intellectual light
Will lay the flesh with nails.
And it will keep the world bright
And closed the body's soft jails.

And from this fair edifice
I shall see, as my eyes blaze,
The moral grandeur of man
Animating all his days.

And peace will marry purpose,
And purity married to grace
Will make the human absolute
As sweet as the human face.

Until my hard vision blears,
And Poverty and Death return
In organ music like the years,
Making the spirit leap, and burn

For the hard intellectual light
That kills all delight
And brings the solemn, inward pain
Of truth into the heart again.

'MY BONES FLEW APART'

My bones flew apart. They flew to the sky,
And as great knockers knocked the air.
The bone God said, Come in,
My soul flew in small and dry.

It is the vale of lamentation,
He said, where Peace never comes,
I thought it was the end for ever
And the forgiving song of no tone.

I was big with thick desire,
I had love like leopard's love,
Time was, time is, time will be,
But see me change I cried horrified

And these dead parts, as dead birds
Tried now wings new and tireless
Winging the fine strife of life
And sudden strength all blind and wry.

We are in the kingdom of awe
My bones cried, my bones sanctified
That blood and bitten mind ne'er dealt
And a cold mist arose around

And the God sighing: I am fiction
I am Intellectual Fruition
Forever a folder open of portals,
The eerie trial of infinite tears

Till my spirit, gasping and sunk
Bereaved of all complexity
When the sun came surging, shook
Back into its knitted unison

Then truth is but simplicity
I cried, revivified, sanctified
And turning to my neighbour alive
Said, I will give my life to you.

THE TRANSFER

Jumping from the certain earth, the river so
Exciting me with the speed of ice and thaw,
From all that solid is, to that which flows,
And spring was in my blood lusty witchery,
It floated before me, island of all excellence,
Crystalline in purity and rarity,
Carried in a slow and bold magnificence
Along the coursing and the swirling river
Like muscles flexing in the backs bent
Of million members of humanity,
A carriage huge, and in that a casket,
Lapped with wavelets tinkling, thence tossed back
By bright and diamond hardness of the gem;
In which I saw the visionary gleam.
And saw my desires fixed in that erected ice
Like giants standing still with mighty eyes,
So alive they had achieved full solitude,
Forms immovable, calm and unassailable,
Whose ruddy breasts breathed the river's rhythm
And their flesh flashed a radiating energy
Shimmering the finely humming air of April,
Then I stood dazzled in an ecstasy
Knowing waste and loss were overborne.
And now my blood so fiercely burned with desire

All was in me lightness elevation and love
While the air's silk beams could bruise
Fingers so keen, though like a steel blade
They would cut the fibrous element between,
Feeling the fine white edges of the ice,
Wherein embodied power and wisdom stood.
Action suspended above both evil and good.

And the ladened river its impending gift
Flowed into my eyes nearer and yet nearer,
Bore onward toward the bank on which I stood;
And when it loomed before me like reality,
I leaped, and a clashing thrashing of the waters
Sent the white ship toward the middle deep
As I crouched in humility, shaking with dread
My being feeling a strangeness like electricity,
The exultation of a world outgrown,
As when a sick man comes to health again.
And as the clear spirit, riding on existence pure,
Lifts its eyes unto the unfathomable blue.
I slipped inside the ice, avid, and put on
Transparency like a flawless feeling of myself
And I saw the world no more as it is
But I had become the vision of my desires,
The island of ice, the ship, the casket, and gem,
Floating on the teeming river's force,
Standing statuesque in the shape of man,
Heroic in the virtue and the power that I adored.
Hour, hour, hour I so flowed.
Time has no running, and it runs not away;
Realisation of being is unchanging felicity;
Desire fulfilled, the end of human action,
Releases in the deep dream of contemplation
The natal awareness of eternal harmony,
And I had longed to leap from solid land
Upon the river that bore ideality,
And felt my brotherhood with heroic men.

Serenely down wide water through the land,
The cake of ice its silent progress making,
See me in the flawless veils of ice
That strange monument, that lifted shape,
That powerful tower in iridescence gleaming,
And though the river moves, I feel no pulse.
She rode in triumph. But the light pierced in,
Shimmering to a flag of gliding colours
And these shivering chimed frostily together
Like swords clashing, kindling spells of music;
Creating pressures, a stealthy sense of dread.
The sun leaned down upon the middle sky,
Then I felt a cleaving, a shiver, a shock,
And like the crumbling of a sheet of cliff
A slab of sliding ice split off and sank.
I looked outward startled, feeling my body's pain,
The opening of a wound that cannot heal,
Like loss of a limb to one who feels it still,
Another rhythm, a breast of the ice tore loose,
Canting into the waves with slipping ease,
The river gathered, the sun pressed closer down
The river began to churn with struggling waves
A stroke like lightning hit and stripped from the body
The last thin scales and brittle veils of ice
Then I, in this cold pitfall snared,
With nervy grip, grasping the raft of ice,
Saw the monstrous passage of the world,
Naked I walked the small confines of hope.
Panic was in me, sickness and clawing death
And like a feverish animal in a cage
I walked forward and then backward frantic,
Another piece of the ice cracked off, another,
Until I had bare room to stand upon.
The land no hope for now; cruel land, she loomed
Like loss, like ruction, like a great prize,
And must for this extreme mistake I pay
(My feet ache, my hands sting, my blood

32

Congeals in fear immense and caged hatred)
With my whole life, drowned in the swirling tide?
There was a little quicker pace in the river,
A dissonance of the unequal stress and strain
Of eddies in the flood, I turned backward
And I saw the force no man can stop
The river looming sullen and uncontrollable
And coming with an ever faster motion
And clashing, hissing, and with massive turmoil
It bore in a vicious surging on again
And I turned forward again livid in panic
I saw the whole force of the mighty surge
Caught in a gigantic breach of clashing,
A whirlpool churning tons of cracking ice
And as the ice I stood on gathered impetus
The baleful scene froze on my mind, I saw
Ice cakes like shapes of a ghastly ocean
Like living men reach up in air
Some with cumbersome motion poised in air
Before they slid down under the tortured mass
While others cracked to bits on the seething surface
Dashed in fragments over the frozen dam
To the slithering downward chaos, abyss delirious
I heard the gashing, slashing of fierce souls,
The quaking shrieking chorus of destruction,
And the eerie sound beyond the world.

Threre was a tree that hung from out the bank
Austere, as if it were a living man.
An arm he held over the flood, and as my craft
Leaped, shivering into death, I leaped to life.

REQUEST FOR OFFERING

Loose the baleful lion, snap
The frosty bars down from his cage
And unclasp the virgin pap
Of the white world to his rage.

See the innocent breast deny
But the bellowing shake down the air
Shudders of passion out of the sky
To shock, mangle and maim, tear.

Under the actual talons see
Virginal white and the black paw
Poised to slash on mystery
The five hates of a claw.

Amaze your eyes now, hard
Is the marble pap of the world
And the baleful lion regard
With the claws of the paw curled.

Loose the baleful lion, snap
The frosty bars down from his cage
And unclasp the virgin pap
Of the white world to his rage.

NECESSITY

See her austere beauty bend;
And her desperate eyes are still.
She walks in terror. And the deep fear
Fascinates me under her will.
The full power of nature unfolds,
Using her like a blind seed.
Now in the awful stillness, watch,
She walks with a panther's need,

Destruction, immediate, violent!
But her lips are livid and chill.
When will the hurt mouth quiver,
The great agony break, and lie still?

Look into her sober eyes, they
Coil sorrow; but the grown malice
Will not spend. There is no hope
To-morrow any hope can be.
It is too late to will; and time
Will blunder its bold meaning
Into her blood, deeper, and more deep,
Then plunder. Be away;
You will not dare her then,
To see the coils of hate uncoil
And the wrought bitterness snap
Free. Go into the woods
And praise the inhuman sun;
Unless wells strangely in you
Pity. The woman will make
The blind cells not to grow.

There is not anything to be sure of,
If destiny will destroy or will build;
And there is nothing to be learned of love
That will not suffer change, or be killed.
We are always about to be used
And are used by nature, without escape,
Save that our wills are with hers fused
And we would impregnate her with our shape.
But in the great moments of being, something
Beyond our wills, is the prime mover
And we do not deny this when we bring
Passionate love to a woman, as a lover;
Since we are compelled by a hid purpose
We cannot control, if joyful or morose.

It is a terrible thrall to be alone,
With all joy there, and destroying fate
Slicing the flesh, hot fangs on the bone;
The intense quality of desire
Blasphemes, and it is at fault to the core.
Silence in bitterness is the hardest thing;
But nobler to ask the fire to burn more,
If the mind can endure, and can sing.
Even beyond joy and despair are spun
Unutterable remoteness in the air,
Intolerable nearness in the sun,
And the separateness of each man in his lair.

THE SCARF OF JUNE

I do not feel spring's windy ingress
In the thickets of my heart
For yet still winter with breast-bands
Of ice, imprisons me.
I slumber through time's weariness,
Apart from phantoms, far apart
From sun's young running down warm lands
With flame for flower and tree.

But when my roots must cringe and thrill
Feeling sharp heat dig down in earth,
My heart will only, leaping, kiss
June's woven scarf that strangled me.
Spirit that animates man and hill
Will work in me hot seasonal birth,
But I, insensible to this,
Will like a cold stone be.

Thus time can do no harm, so let
Him come, through roots and branches creeping,
Bringing spring and winter in
And hurrying life away.

For I am where no sun shone yet,
And am earth's inner being keeping,
Locked in this lone discipline
Against the world's decay.

EXPERIENCE EVOKED

Now come to me all men
With savagery and innocence,
With axe to chop the fir tree,
Or seed, small, for the immense
Sewing of earth with old Rose.
Now come all men, arrayed
With the colours of the garden
Around them where they stayed
Till bone began to harden
Under the thinning of the nose.
Come all men, unto whom
Wind was a snarling wire whip
In the contusions of a doom
And with red flecks on their lip
They leaped up, danced, grew tall.
Come all, the babe bound
In terror and panic cry;
Or an old man found
With a skylark in his eye.
Come, harsh shroud over all.

TWO LOVES

That her serene influence should spread
An afternoon of soft autumnal light
Is to my heart not unaccountable
For she was young, and is not dead.
And still her cheek is red and white.

But that this stealthy still insistent power
Pervades my mind and will not slumber me
Is delicate woe and glory hard to bear;
Her life lives in a ghost-wrought hour,
From whose chill spirit I am not free.

The one was willow to an ardent touch
And she was mood that had a right to die.
But she, the other, the passion of my mind
Long-living still, does overmuch
Come from the dead, and from the sky.

BURDEN

Whoever lives beside a mountain knows,
Although he dares not speak it out, that he
Must always carry on his heart the snows
That burden down the trees. And never the sea
Will rush around him cool, like snow-cool air,
And carry him and lift him like a leaf.
He will not find this lightness anywhere
Since mountains brood, they hold dark league with grief.

The pine trees never tire of moving down
The slopes to meet him, pointing up from town
Beyond the tree-line to the rigid peaks.
The mountain holds him though it never speaks.
He scrambles over boulders on his knees
Trying to reach the summit, like the trees.

'IN PRISONS OF ESTABLISHED CRAZE'

In prisons of established craze
Hear the sane tread without noise
Whose songs no iron walls will raze
Though hearts are as of girls or boys.

By the waters burning clear
Where sheds of men are only seen,
Accept eloquent time, and revere
The silence of the great machine.
On the sweet earth green and moist
When vainglorious cities magnify,
The senseless dissonance will foist
As witless on the shining sky.
There is some stealth in rhythm yet
Albeit an even breath is not.
In the mind is a gauge set,
Lest the blood spill, and blot.

THE LARGESS

With cicada's nymphal skin
So have I meetings made,
Let down my eyes to him,
With fear upon that thin shade.

Lest the look I gave
Was death's loving me,
To every memory have,
That himself he see.

Yet O marvellous crispness,
Dun, but perfect structure,
Thin as matter is,
It has its wondrous lure.

And took it in my grassy feel,
That cold, that final form,
If still it be the same;
Alert to a hoped harm.

Where have you gone, slight being
Whose brown monument

Mirror makes of wings
Yet in a damp tenement.

Can I among winds lose you
When vibrant is all air?
Must I not use you
Then in every desire?

Do treble drums a changing
Ecstasy keep fresh;
Insistent, sing to me,
Over fields of August.

It has not denied my mind,
But no sign has made,
Bleak, delicate, defined
And crinkled husk once life had.

My eyes soothe over him,
My hand trembles with force.
What eternal hovers in
Him: speak, are you corpse?

'WHEN DORIS DANCED'

When Doris danced under the oak tree
The sun himself might wish to see,
Might bend beneath those lovers, leaves,
While her her virgin step she weaves
And envious cast his famous hue
To make her daft, yet win her too.

When Doris danced under the oak tree
Slow John, so stormed in heart, at sea
Gone all his store, a wreck he lay.
But on the ground the sun-beams play.
They lit his face in such degree
Doris lay down, all out of pity.

'THE CRITIC WITH HIS PAINED EYE'

The critic with his pained eye
Cannot my source espy
For truly and purely to eye it
He would have as Critic to die.

I with joyful vision see,
I cannot his purpose acquire.
For if the Critic were truly free
He would love, and not be a liar.

THE YOUNG HUNTER

Here gunned he homeward in the birdy breast;
Muscles full of baskets spread a picnic.
Let the palping trickle, the wing's blood's best
Be, as it was, his hunting heart's quick.

And I allude a mary-gold's guts
Are no match, brass heart, for yours.
Nor dug themselves in magnifying ruts
Where passes to repast, hulk that stirs.

Observe the revel of the nerveless finger.
Praise the young; lo, praise the dead.
It changed none the mysterious transfer
That long since knelled a questing in the head.

'WHEN GOLDEN FLIES UPON MY CARCASS COME'

When golden flies upon my carcass come,
Those pretty monsters, shining globules
Like tautened oily suns, and congregate
Fixing their several gems upon one core
That shines a blossom then of burning gold,

41

'Tis as the sun's burning glass and diadem
They work, at the first chance of rotten flesh,
And, senseless little messengers of time,
Some beauty keep even at the guts of things,
Which is a fox caught, and I watch the flies.

'NOW IS THE AIR MADE OF CHIMING BALLS'

Now is the air made of chiming balls.
The stormcloud, wizened, has rolled its rind away.
Now is the eye with hill and valley laved
And the seeds, assuaged, peep from the nested spray.
The bluebird drops from a bough. The speckled meadow-lark
Springs in his lithe array. Fresh air
Blesses the vanished tear; the bunched anguish.
The laughing balls their joyful pleasure tear.
Renewed is the whole world and the sun
Begins to dress with warmth again every thing.
The lettuce in pale burn; the burdock tightening;
And naked necks of craning fledglings.

THE CHILD

Five years of cringing child small,
Bewildered by the barren wall.
Laughed Atlantic its heated summer,
This I do not remember.
O the fearful cliff wall,
And the fearful sapling nigh.
And the dove that will hurt me,
And the great hand of the sky.

'LET THE TIGHT LIZARD ON THE WALL'

Let the tight lizard on the wall
No green spike see: but tickled eyes
Sparkle up at the sun's dazzle,
Lungs, lithe, strike no sigh.

So to be instant adamant,
Pipped, a nimbus exhales,
Of exquisite leaf-lave,
And he contains time's fail.

And he durst himself absorb,
The canker pelts to defy,
Blot of dark he to exude,
That marriage of the sky.

Quiver no joy to me, I see
The world grown too delicate.
I grieve thy black skeleton,
Still overlayed by fate.

O could I delve thy shimmer,
Such forth thy shiver, and for
All time clasp the answer,
What protection, who the protector.

'I WENT TO SEE IRVING BABBITT'

I went to see Irving Babbitt
In the Eighteenth Century clean and neat
When he opened his mouth to speak French
I fell clean off my seat.

He spoke it not fair and fetisly
But harshly laboured it like a Yankee

Even as my nubian Swahili
Is sweet and pleasant to me.

And when we went out of the critical door
Crying for more, crying for more
I saw the hater of mechanical America
Bulge through the Square in a critical Ford.

Harvard is a good place, Harvard is the best,
Among the immemorial elms you'll come to rest
Strolling the Yard, the only proper yardstick,
Warbling your native foot-notes mild.

RECOLLECTION OF CHILDHOOD

O the jungle is beautiful the jungle is wild
Here are the rodents and the butterflies,
The thorn tree prickles and the shady grottoes,
And I'll lie in the sun all day, and the shade.

And here is the orchard, bulging big fruit,
Adazzle in the eyes all red and golden,
There is the barn, and the many cows,
Hurray for the hay, I'll fall and tumble in the hay.

And below the happy pasture green and moist
I'll walk it to the shady grove by the river,
Swim the clear stream, the chalk cliff climb,
Bursting with desire still—cease action never,

But in the natural world of happy forms
Bird, beast, tree, fern, earth and rain and sun
Live melodious love, and touch above
All fingered air the very god of love.

ORCHARD

I

Lovely were the fruit trees in the evening.
We sat in the automobile all five of us,
Full of the silence of deep grieving,
For tragedy stalked among the fruit trees.

Strongest was the father, of solid years,
Who set his jaw against the coming winter,
Pure, hard, strong, and infinitely gentle
For the worst that evil brings can only kill us.

Most glorious was the mother, beautiful
Who in the middle course of life was stalked
By the stark shape of malignant disease,
And her face was holy white like all desire.

And we three, in our benumbing youngness,
Half afraid to guess at the danger there,
Looked in stillness at the glowing fruit trees,
While tumultuous passions raged in the air.

II

And the first, the father, with indomitable will
Strove in iron decision, in all human strength
With a powerful complete contempt of defeat,
Six feet of manhood and not a mark of fear.

And the next, the mother, wonderfully mild,
Wise with the wisdom that never changes,
Poured forth her love divinely magnified
We knew not by what imminent despair.

While the older brother and the younger,
Separate, yet placed in the first light

Of brutal recognition, held a trembling sister
Who knew not the trial of fortitude to come.

And in the evening, among the warm fruit trees
All of life and all of death were there,
Of pain unto death, of struggle to endure,
And the strong right of human love was there.

THE SOUL LONGS TO RETURN
WHENCE IT CAME

I drove up to the graveyard, which
Used to frighten me as a boy,
When I walked down the river past it,
And evening was coming on. I'd make sure
I came home from the woods early enough.
I drove in, I found to the place, I
Left the motor running. My eyes hurried,
To recognize the great oak tree
On the little slope, among the stones.
It was a high day, a crisp day,
The cleanest kind of Autumn day,
With brisk intoxicating air, a
Little wind that frisked, yet there was
Old age in the atmosphere, nostalgia,
The subtle heaviness of the Fall.
I stilled the motor. I walked a few paces;
It was good, the tree; the friendliness of it.
I touched it, I thought of the roots;
They would have pierced her seven years.
O all peoples! O mighty shadows!
My eyes opened along the avenue
Of tombstones, the common land of death.
Humiliation of all loves lost,
That might have had full meaning in any
Plot of ground, come, hear the silence,
See the quivering light. My mind worked

Almost imperceptibly, I
In the command, I the wilful ponderer.
I must have stood silent and thoughtful
There. A host of dry leaves
Danced on the ground in the wind.
They startled, they curved up from the ground,
There was a dry rustling, rattling.
The sun was motionless and brittle.
I felt the blood darken in my cheeks
And burn. Like running. My eyes
Telescoped on decay, I out of command.
Fear, tenderness, they seized me.
My eyes were hot, I dared not look
At the leaves. A pagan urge swept me.
Multitudes, O multitudes in one.
The urge of the earth, the titan
Wild and primitive lust, fused
On the ground of her grave.
I was a being of feeling alone.
I flung myself down on the earth
Full length on the great earth, full length,
I wept out the dark load of human love.
In pagan adoration I adored her.
I felt the actual earth of her.
Victor and victim of humility,
I closed in the wordless ecstasy
Of mystery: where there is no thought
But feeling lost in itself forever,
Profound, remote, immediate, and calm.
Frightened, I stood up, I looked about
Suspiciously, hurriedly (a rustling),
As if the sun, the air, the trees
Were human, might not understand.
I drew breath, it made a sound,
I stepped gingerly away. Then
The mind came like a fire, it
Tortured man, I thought of madness.

47

The mind will not accept the blood.
The sun and sky, the trees and grasses,
And the whispering leaves, took on
Their usual characters. I went away,
Slowly, tingling, elated, saying, saying
Mother, Great Being, O Source of Life
To whom in wisdom we return,
Accept this humble servant evermore.

GRAVE PIECE

The lustral sweat in its fine slow beads,
Loosed from the massive burning brow,

    (I try something new, I break my skull.
    Death, I try to get into you.)

Bit drills, bit little axes, like heavenly saws
Through sunshine, incrassated on the stone,

    (I make a picture-map a process,
    For the instruction of logicians.)

The glassy lapses of uncloven time.
In, tender; in, bitter; in, indifferent,
The shiny spheres their nakedness assail,
Tiny wanton world revelling joyers,

    (Death comes in the whirlwind, or like a cat,
    Death creeps down like a suspiration,
    Because I have life Death is Death
    And through Death I try to reach perfection.)

Seepers; and spread a frostwork hands
There in the vasy tomb of bone-green icicles,
And gelid grasses of cold bruise to touch;
Of looking roots, night agate eyed; and

(Love is in me, love Protean
Strange and potent, as the stone uncloven.
And all the sunny afternoon of summertime
Think, wink, entombed, feel, steal)

Lynx-lensed weeds' fixed-pricking stare,
And air with motion scarce as sight
Above born squinting flowers, screaming, frozen,
Composed in a scenic breakage of blear light

(Love flooding me, I would overcome the world
I must discover inexorable Death,
Death and Imagination conjoining—
—tickling gnat my fingers flies from)

To static points and rays of endless sameness,
The things themselves, their fatal natures;
And the syzygy caused a stony sound
Through hollow, skull-shaped geology,

(Attempting to do what cannot be done,
Poetry to break the marble word
Even as time sullied the carven name,
And I am trying to fly through Death like a bird.)

And from this I saw grow
Although my sense shook with fear
A crystal Tear
Whose centre is spiritual love.

THE HUMANIST

Hunting for the truly human
I looked for the true man
And saw an ape at the fair
With the circle still to square. Learning
Breeds its own ignorance. Fame and power

49

Demand a rush and pounding.
Those who rush through rush through, and who
Are they but those who rush through?
Yet truth resides in contemplation
And comprehension of contemplation
Not necessarily of Plato. Action explains
A field full of folk and golden football flexions,
Action for actors. Truth through contemplation
Resurrects the truly human,
Makes known the true man
Whom these lines can scan:
But miss his secret final point.
The world is too much in joint. No use
Setting that right, that squaring, that harrying: for
The true man lives in mystery
Of God; God his agile soul will see
But he will not see God's majesty,
And that is what makes you and me
Whether man or woman
Neither true nor free
But truly human.

THE VIRGIN

I will not think of her in her coffin
With worms' teeth needling a death's head
In her red, and white, and soft cheek;
Her resilient hair, crushed dead,
That only the boy winds fingered.
The virginal nipples pinched by stones.
The silver belly sullied by slime,
Kiss unreciprocate; bones, O!
Without strength to round the womb.
And April skin-shine browned and fouled.
Stinking under the sweating earth,
The mind's whole marble disembowled.
Save me these pictures, you denisens,

Captain worms of the gross earth,
That I may tear from my mind such album,
Formal decay: death's hideous birth.
No better than a beggar, a base
Whore, or baser, a designing lecher;
Equal to Helen, diced with jewels,
Putrid at the bawdy event, like her.
My poor Moll, dead as a stump,
It's good I knew you not, sweet,
But in feeling's jammed proximity;
Doltish memory, cranky perception
Give you the lie, for my brain sue,
While, mured up in this ruinous vision,
My mind beats lively as a disease.

'MAN'S GREED AND ENVY ARE SO GREAT'

Man's greed and envy are so great
He'll go to any length or date
To beat down his fellow man,
If beat him down he can.

Though under dread he cower,
He'll do it in the name of power
That obvious, that visible success
Prove to the world his canniness.

And let Christ go; let Truth
Hang; praise the fang and the tooth,
Force life though like a balling youth,
The truant animal in action.

Praise to the thinkers and the dreamers
Those dear quaint saintly creatures.
They evade the blood to build the brain,
Philosophic men who love the sun.

The goal of intellectual man
Striving to do what he can
To bring down out of uncreated light
Illumination to our night

Is not possession of the fire
Annihilation of his own desire
To the source a secret soaring
And all his self outpouring

Nor is it an imageless place
Wherein there is no human face
Nor laws, nor hierarchies, nor dooms
And only the cold weight of the tomb

But it is human love, love
Concrete, specific, in a natural move
Gathering goodness, it is free
In the blood as in the mind's harmony,

It is love discoverable here
Difficult, dangerous, pure, clear,
The truth of the positive hour
Composing all of human power.

'IF I COULD ONLY LIVE AT THE PITCH THAT IS NEAR MADNESS'

If I could only live at the pitch that is near madness
When everything is as it was in my childhood
Violent, vivid, and of infinite possibility:
That the sun and the moon broke over my head.

Then I cast time out of the trees and fields,
Then I stood immaculate in the Ego;
Then I eyed the world with all delight,
Reality was the perfection of my sight.

And time has big handles on the hands,
Fields and trees a way of being themselves.
I saw battalions of the race of mankind
Standing stolid, demanding a moral answer.

I gave the moral answer and I died
And into a realm of complexity came
Where nothing is possible but necessity
And the truth wailing there like a red babe.

'I WALKED OUT TO THE GRAVEYARD TO SEE THE DEAD'

I walked out to the graveyard to see the dead
The iron gates were locked, I couldn't get in,
A golden pheasant on the dark fir boughs
Looked with fearful method at the sunset,

Said I, Sir bird, wink no more at me
I have had enough of my dark eye-smarting,
I cannot adore you, nor do I praise you,
But assign you to the rafters of Montaigne.

Who talks with the Absolute salutes a Shadow,
Who seeks himself shall lose himself;
And the golden pheasants are no help
And action must be learned from love of man.

A MEDITATION

Now you are holding my skull in your hand.
I am not anybody. I am dead.
God has taken my life away. You are holding
My skull in your hand, the wind is blowing
(Blowing, the ineffable structure of the wind)
The wind is blowing through my skull like a horn
And you are thinking of the world's unearthly music
And of the beauty beyond the earth and seas,
You think the tune will tell you of the truth,
You are thinking: thinking, are you?—are you
Thinking? I am dead. I am dead and in your hand.

Now what does it matter whether I lived or died
Or when I lived or when I died or what I tried
To do of all the things there are to do in the world,
You might be musing upon a finch, or a melon,
You might be not you but somebody else, some other,
Some utter muser, maybe, in some other land
With some other kind of brains or bones, or both,
Some lack of bile to make these peregrinations;
You might be a man who never found me at all,
That miraculous fellow, that idoitic genius
Who never had to think of the wind in my skull at all.

There, you see I am so helpless in your hands.
I cannot get back, cannot reach or yearn back,
Nor summon love enough, nor the intellectual care—
Being dead, you talk as if I had spirit at all—
To come back to you and tell you who I am.
You do me too much honour with your grave words

And quizzical head bent down, trace of a lovable smile,
Too much too much honour for one so windless,
And witless, wizened long past wandering and pondering.
Go back to your strict duties of the earth, man,
Make love to your girl long nights, and long summer days.

But there, you hold me, a philosopher! If philosophical,
You had better put me back in the earth,
Hold nothing at all! Hold your own hand, man!
Now you can feel the dainty wind playing through it
Weaving among your fingers what you want to know.
There is the place to love and make your contemplations
For you can still make your fingers fly and go.
Of all symbols the cunning mind devises
None can be so strict, so purely right
As the hand that makes the fingers fashion the love
Contending in immaterial mastery.

But something touches you, deeply, beyond all comment,
Something so tender, wise, human; you are only human
And grief makes you as a little child that weeps
For you do not know why you are in the world
Nor how you got here, in any real sense, nor how long
Before some ruthless shock will end you forever,
That peculiar you you must cherish, the uniqueness,
The kind not like the skull that is in your hand
But that is fixed in its intricate nicety,—
As who can imagine, seeing a fine bull in pasture
That that magnificent creature will lie down and die?

God has taken my life away. I am dead,
I am not anybody. I am no oracle. You be
An oracle, if you can. You be full of imagination.
You see beyond me, which is seeing beyond yourself,
Yours is the purely human burden and the prophecy.
These things can only be talked of by men.
Man is the talking machine; or the arcane marionette

Who like a god thinks himself to be immune
From the terrible void and absolute darkness
The unthinkable loss and final destitution
Upon which he builds (O! yes!) his mighty hierarchies.

But if I had the power to seem to be,
Or could even wish to be powerful, and say
'I am Lord of Life. I am Eternal Life'—
I could not say it, the contradiction is too great.
This goes too far, and lacks a certain humour.
You build a fiction of what I am, or could be,
And amidst the limits of your mentality and words
Revolve, with all your feelings stumbling blocks
And your keenest thoughts barbs of fiery wire.
O dear sweet little timeful poor creature
Tell this skull what it cares not to say

Life blows like the wind away

You have run the weirs of the emotions,
Even as I did; but they are not through with you yet.
There will be many complicated messages,
Memory will make of your heart a veritable mill,
The need for action jerk your legs, ambition
Choke you, rage consume you almost to inanition,
Conquest will thrill you, and defeat annul you.
And you will not have enough, but lust of life
Drive you on to the cold, very brink of the grave
With man's old captive, cyclic wish to know
What it is all about, meaning and moral dimension.

What is it all about, you are asking me now
For it is less of me than of yourself you are thinking,
Surely more of yourself, flesh-bound as you are—
You would withdraw in horror at my secret,
You would not want to know, your long-lashed eyes aglare,
Of the cold absolute blankness and fate of death,

Of the depths of being beyond all words to say,
Of your profound or of the world's destiny,
Of the mind of God, rising like a mighty fire
Pure and calm beyond all mortal instances
Magnificent, eternal, Everlasting, sweet and mild.

No, I rise a little, I come to life a little.
If I could only make you see the simple truth,
So simple it is so hard to say, hard to believe,
That you are to be man, that is, to be human,
You are imperfect, will never know perfection,
You must strive, but the goal will recede forever,
That you must do what the great poets and the sages say,
Obeying scripture even in the rotten times,
That you must, also, not think nor feel too much
(For the Greeks knew what they were talking about),
And that, as you have lived, so must you die

And blow like the wind away

Now you walk back among the flowers of the world.
You have put me down and I am myself again.
Now you return, return from your solemn meditation
Among the strange shadows, the strange veils of longing
And through the cathartic action of beautiful contemplation
Seek among your fellow creatures whatever is good in life,
Purified by this; for, as sin purifies lust,
As war purges society, as death rarifies life,
So the contemplation of death is valuable
Restorative of the soul to new even reaches
Easing a little the burden of our suffering

Before we blow like the wind away

And blow like the wind away

'THE FULL OF JOY DO NOT KNOW; THEY NEED NOT'

The full of joy do not know; they need not
Know. Nothing is reconciled.
They flash the light of Heaven indeed.
Let them have it, let them have it, it is mild.

Those who suffer see the truth; it has
Murderous edges. They never avert
The gaze of calculation one degree,
But they are hurt, they are hurt, they are hurt.

RUMINATION

When I can hold a stone within my hand
And feel time make it sand and soil, and see
The roots of living things grow in this land,
Pushing between my fingers flower and tree,
Then I shall be as wise as death,
For death has done this and he will
Do this to me, and blow his breath
To fire my clay, when I am still.

'COVER ME OVER'

Cover me over, clover;
Cover me over, grass.
The mellow day is over
And there is night to pass.

Green arms about my head,
Green fingers on my hands.
Earth has no quieter bed
In all her quiet lands.

THE RECAPITULATION

Not through the rational mind,
But by elation coming to me
Sometimes, I am sure
Death is but a door.

A state of purity, sweet grace
It is, nor can last long,
But in that essence, I feel
Life beyond death is real.

Perhaps it is only the human need.
When reason rules, reason denies it.
But comes elation unto me
And blows God all through me.

When the flesh was young and strong
And the mind also, I denied God.
But time's sullen call
Has made my body fall.

Spirit of holy love, arise,
Meek and gentle, sweet and calm,
Arise in the ruthless world
And your truth put on.

To the rational mind grant
Things rational. But to the spirit
(All things there possible)
Accord what is spiritual.

'IMAGINING HOW IT WOULD BE
TO BE DEAD'

Imagining how it would be to be dead,
Until my tender filaments
From mere threads air have become
And this is all my consciousness

(While like a world of rock and stone
My body cumbersome and big
Breathes out a vivid atmosphere
Which is the touchless breach of the air)
I lost my head, and could not hold
Either my hands together or my heart
But was so sentient a being
I seemed to break time apart
And thus became all things air can touch
Or could touch could it touch all things,
And this was an embrace most dear,
Final, complete, a flying without wings.
From being bound to one poor skull,
And that surrounded by one earth,
And the earth in one universe forced,
And that chained to some larger gear,
I was the air, I was the air,
And then I pressed on eye and cheek
The sightless hinges of eternity
That make the whole world creak.

'I WALKED OVER THE GRAVE
OF HENRY JAMES'

I walked over the grave of Henry James
But recently, and one eye kept the dry stone.
The other leaned on boys at games away,
My soul was balanced in my body cold.

I am one of those prodigals of hell
Whom ten years have seen cram with battle;
Returns to what he canted from, grants it good,
As asthma makes itself a new resolution.

I crushed a knob of earth between my fingers,
This is a very ordinary experience.
A name may be glorious but death is death,
I thought, and took a street-car back to Harvard Square.

THE INEFFABLE

When Eve ate the apple
My woes began,
But I didn't believe then
That I would believe in Original Sin.
When Adam delved
I began to fail,
But I didn't comprehend
The majesty of the Supra Rational.

That Cain and Abel
Should be such brothers
And not love each other
Seemed not in the nature of things.
These were old fables
Of the dimly understood,
When man began to construct
Evil and Good.

Than the passion of pied air
Flew through the days,
The days used the years,
The years grew to tears—
Logic made the stories go
And imagination moved the key.
Somewhere Love came in,
Quietly, mysteriously.

The force as odd as any
After all is said
Has more sense in it
Than hounding the dead.
And the bond of the obvious
Blood in its beauty
Controls more, is not moral,
Simply is.

When nothing can be understood,
World-systems crumble,
Love is of the essence,
Poetically speaking.
As in music
The truth is in between the tones,
Neither action nor will
Tell what is going on;
It is something glancing off
Allures always,
The rich sense
Of the all, the impossible, the ineffable.

'MYSTICISM HAS NOT THE PATIENCE TO WAIT FOR GOD'S REVELATION'

KIERKEGAARD

But to reach the archimedean point
Was all my steadfastness;
The disjointed times to teach
Courage from what is dreadful.

It was the glimpses in the lightning
Made me a sage, but made me say
No word to make another fight,
My own fighting heart full of dismay.

Spirit, soul, and fire are reached!
And springs of the mind, like springs of the feet
Tell all, all know, nothing wavers there!
All the flowers of the heart turn to ice-flowers,

Heaviness of the world prevailing
('The higher we go the more terrible it is')
Duplicity of man, heart-hate,
The hypocrite, the vain, the whipper, the cheat,

The eternal ape on the leash,
Drawing us down to faith,
Which the Greeks call divine folly,
The tug of laughter and of irony.

THE DREAM

In a dream I was in a tunnel struggling
A chalky tunnel, and torturous place,
With at the end a suggestion of light,
A space of light and gruff old optimistic strokes
For though convulsed, frisked, I felt I would reach the light

And as in a dream things happen without pain,
In a childhood sequence of untractable reality,
In this pleasurable though unpredictable predicament
I struggled, drawn directly by the great light,
The tunnel was merely there, exfoliating.

Then as if angels whisked you, an unseen force
Yet seemingly not a force, for all was fervent balance,
I was in high regions of beautiful world and life,
I visited the extreme palaces, stroked the glowing air,
Went up through hitched forests to a gold plateau

And all was triumph, magnitude, deep vistas,
All was largest of harmonies, freedom of form,
Luminous periodicities in a static realm,
The unimaginable godhead, divine peculiarity,
The child's, the death's-head's unconquerable vanity.

THE MOMENT OF VISION

The moment of vision will come when it will,
The gift of the gods, the unshakable
Unbreakable
Subtle intuitive stewardship, and still
That matchless satisfaction of the maker.

63

To read the spirit was all my care and is,
To lose life to find hope,
To destroy in the heady grope
For new worlds upon an old's effacement,
Through the breach of evil the breath of grace.

Those men who fight for the spirit have my love,
Fierce young poets tearing their hearts out,
Strong for many materialistic bouts,
Destroyers who put on creation like a glove,
Wear grace from their despair: the wrenched fist.

The worthy one who did a worthier thing
Than all the worthies did—he kept that hid;
Him whom another age heard not,
But now my surest music of the word,
Earth-thrown singer, who burnt his bridges.

RETROSPECTIVE FORELOOK

The logical pleasure of expectant mercy
Will be an end of us, will make an end.
The demon pulling us from the peach orchard
Where we were uninfected, ineffectual in time,
Cannot get off our skins; we did not win,
But entered more fully the manhood of sin.

The book of Boehme, being tired after bicycling,
The visionary voluptuary asleep in the hay,
All that effort in the fresh fields of the French,
These were days were prayers were potent maskers,
Fame on his forehead, the gust a good gear,
Where now the glory of the ghostly year?

Pascal, too, the attic full of strife and charm,
Mozart a checkerwork of lilacs; Descartes,
Who in his statue, strangely singular in Tours,
Set the savage mirror in the delving eye,

These were pilgrims come to country new
To pommel, hearten, sing, seem, and sue.

The old vexation of the moon! Climbing Chartres,
Where on the windy roof, midst gargoyles intricate,
What moonlight and what noonday imaginings
Compelled the reason and made dim the blood
In shadows of the past over the champaign
In silent noonlong or roan night of rain.

While in that vault where mostly man makes God,
The hallowed light at evening dimly falls,
(the dimness of the nave gravely the light recalls)
But falling brings the glow and golden growth
Of vague, supernatural, spiritual pressures
where the weight of our redemption seems
A compilation of and nurse of dreams.

And long were days and tall were tremble-trees,
The symbol of the self lost in a haze.
And errors of sentience, O senses sweet! sour! sweet!
That ravelled out your substance quizzically,
To go forward and to retreat, to gain
And lose, and never to quite see the truth plain!

That struggle of all Europe! The massive English means
Contiguous to reason, lapsed in jiggly greens,
Where heart was pierced, harrowed the head, was bride
To lust of learning, and the whole eye acquist.
There were the centuries a valid looks,
On English faces no need to read the books.

The demon drives us and we have to go.
The dangerous mountains never climbed aspired to,
While tops of standing, dancing places, are descried.
Consciousness it is that blights us all,
Visionary candor in the branches
Hallucinatory avalanche the pandar.

While stealing through the nave so ancient seeming
The truth of metaphysical reason there concordant,
Stark Lenin, radiant, with blood upon his head
And hands like hams that fed a famished land
Was all that subtlety is worth, and more,
Was the West, was what the world would be.

THE LYRIC ABSOLUTE

I

Art, the holy care of life
Excruciate, and the wife
Of love, in sounding strangeness sleeps
Through the wars of the active deep,
And I hear the struggles and wails of desire
Sunk in redemption's purifying fire,
And I am made like a child
Who would not be mild.

II

Images of death arise
And scatter the skies.
Images of life depend
Upon joy in man.
The stars of day fall
And the night arises bleak
And Christ in whole blood
His Child in Man seeks.

'I WILL NOT DARE TO ASK ONE QUESTION'

I will not dare to ask one question.
Fondling the warm sun while I may,
A man married to oblivion
I will kiss her mistress lips all day;
But in this bed the solemn blooms
Of the darkness grow in the bones,
That are a slow drug to the mind.

I will not dare to ask the stones.
One night alone told quietly
How I must move back to the womb
Which nourished me on the unknown
And once more in that love entomb,
Thus, without answer, simply,
Gone, damned, the loam over me.

NEW HAMPSHIRE, FEBRUARY

Nature had made them hide in crevices,
Two wasps so cold they looked like bark.
Why I do not know, but I took them
And I put them
In a metal pan, both day and dark.

Like God touching his finger to Adam
I felt, and thought of Michaelangelo,
For whenever I breathed on them,
The slightest breath,
They leaped, and preened as if to go.

My breath controlled them always quite.
More sensitive than electric sparks
They came into life
Or they withdrew to ice,
While I watched, suspending remarks.

Then one in a blind career got out,
And fell to the kitchen floor. I
Crushed him with my cold ski boot,
By accident. The other
Had not the wit to try or die.

And so the other is still my pet.
The moral of this is plain.
But I will shirk it.
You will not like it. And
God does not live to explain.

TRIPTYCH

PERCY

Whimsicality is a thing in itself.
Cast out your noble argument.
You've only got to go look
At a child fetched forth from the womb,
Or see an old codger croak,
To assume the world is nothing but sorrow.

JOHN

But, you forget, sir,
The importance of values,
Of rigorous discernment among them.

PERCY

Ha, your cheeks will be long
Enough to make sizable culverts
In them, down which to flush
The tearful sorrows of your seriousness.
Come, praise whimsicality.
He's a painted clown can walk a
Tight rope narrowly, and will fool the people.
He's your only modern who can't be criticized.
He's understudy to the true bigwigs,
Those who experience experience.
Mark his moony jaws and craven
Pate, his withal constancy.
Critics be brought to the tent.
They have not learnt all.
They want juice.

JOHN

My dear sir,
You run on like an adolescent litterateur.
Come out of it.
Let us get down to reality—

PERCY
Ho, reality is up. What's up? So
We are up to reality. I
Insist on levity. There's a
Certain deviltry in all levity.
Let your philosophical discourse
Wait on the slow decay of paper.
The shelves will last and the books on them,
Till the digger worms set up a Piccadilly
And haul stuffs hard through the tubes
That the forage of nature's
Dumped atop the sheaves of art.
Spirit won't keep.
But like the laughter in the throat
It shocks out over the teeth
In a stony springing brook;
Falls over an edge and
Becomes an airy gauze;
Becomes great laughing-crystals.
The worms have no guts,
And must eat only wood and paper.
I am Air-eater,
The hardest, rarest occupation.

JOHN
It is time I praised my own tolerance,
But I have known you so long
I will allow you the pleasures of expansion.
However, I have for the past fortnight
Examined the five volumes of the late Dr. Fardel,
The latinist we knew at the University—

PERCY
If you
Would put all the great brains of
Oxford and Cambridge in a tub
And boil them for three and thirty minutes,
You might beget an elf.

69

JOHN

As I was saying, the learned Doctor—

PERCY

Oh—I feel a pun coming.
Hmmm. A gross pun, although
All men hate them, is worth more than
A quire of your syllogistic Doctors.
Is an integer of sense, a compound
Of fertility; albeit an indigestible squib.

JOHN

Spare me your puns anyway.
Now, his theory in general is—

PERCY

I wonder if he theorized in his lady's bed.
No doubt, being a Latin scholar,
He went over old conjugations.

JOHN

This so-called merriment of yours
Is merely dull superstructure
You erect upon your ignorance.

PERCY

If I'm ignorant, then I love ignorance.
I'll squeeze it into a voluptuous guffaw then.
And I'll shout ignorance at you
Until you get some sense.

JOHN

Such a belligerent attitude is hardly
Becoming to one of your formal education.
But in our last discussion, I recall
We had seriously got to the point of—

The point of merriment at you, sir!
When a man is out of work,
And loitering in his father's plush arm-chair,
It's grand to stalk the realistic pessimists.
But I am for the point of ignition:
Let the intellectual hayricks
In the wet season be burnt up by
The sun's hilarious eye.
Asthma has got a grip on existence.
That is my particular gripe. A jape.
In truth, I am so full of glee I am
More ridiculous than before I said so.
Come, now, have you ever seen
A critic jump a fence?
'Twould be damned bad for his criticism.
I'll bet the barbed wire would
Criticize his backside, make him
Bleed out his petty principles;
He should have jumped higher, and got over the Greeks.

JOHN

Well, I guess I must leave you
And go back to my discourses.
You seem incapable of
Even an attempt at lucidity.

PERCY

What, lucidity?
When Lucy is lucid to me
I will tempt her and attempt her
And run and tell thee.
Pardon, I retch. It must be the acidity.

JOHN

You make me sick.

PERCY

Be merry. As long as you are not married,
You might as well be merry.
Really, tomorrow I will cry all day.
I will buy little squirt guns filled
With sugar water and run them down
The two lobes of my face,
To let you know I am crying.
Tomorrow I will be the soul of solemnity.
I will go to the Museum and lie down
Full length in a Medieval stone coffin.
I did it once, and was so grievous a sight,
The attendant broke out laughing.
Let me groan from six o'clock in the morning.
By noon I will have got the habit,
And by night I shall be an absolute wailing ghost.

JOHN

Come, you are not reasonable.

PERCY

Reason and treason are the same thing to me.
Reason is too credulous.
It irks me like old ladies;
Or old gubernatorial gentlemen.
Ha! I fly by Absolute Force.
I am so light the air is my very being
And I would be all over the sky.
Your reasoners only poke about in old clothes.

JOHN

You simply rave against what you love.

PERCY

If I rave against what I love,
You fail me in reciprocal

72

Love of what you hate.
Oh, there comes a she.
Now I must fly against
The earthly quality of women.
Hello, vegetable, how's your green hue?

PRISCILLA

What sport is this?

JOHN

Good afternoon, dear. My greetings. Don't bother
About him; he's in a ripe inconsequence,
And won't bother us a bit. What a lovely frock—

PRISCILLA

I have just come from town with a car
Full of sheer things, the smartest things from Paris.
And these matching jewels from India.

PERCY

Oh, for a new attitude to death.
The Polynesians did well when they
Packed and squeezed the head down to
The round and look of a sick lemon
Left over long in the sun. Fond embalmers.
The bulging fellow got down at last,
Brains confessed in a boy's handful.

PRISCILLA

What an awful fool. How should I
Provoke such language, and with my new ensemble?

JOHN

As host, I must ameliorate
Between your displeasure and his candour.

73

I propose tombstones and mausoleums
Be laid under the pile-driver
And done into powder for the cheeks of virgins.
Such quantities of the stuff would be,
And so few authoritative patronizers,
They'd be chalked to the death withal,
Tricked out with the most emaciated spells
To get their man. Now, these dead.
What to do with the dead. I once saw a
Groundhog stick his fat corpse
Into the very light of July.
It blistered, broke loose, and you've never seen
So merry a sight. Soon he was aswim
In his own oils, hot as a lecher,
And then he was dancing with maggots.
In a fortnight he was itching with
A most greedy dissipation,
As hilarious as a bunch of bees,
And strong enough to drive off a troop of buzzards.
By August middle he had got strained
Into a nervous maniacal gymnastic,
And by December his divine frenzy
Was quits with the world.
I passed by the place the next summer,
It had a lonely look.
Indeed, he had only a little hairy ghost.
But it would boil again; and manure the wild flowers.
Now take corpses, stretch them out
In bold capable nakedness
On the ground and see them do likewise.
And liveliness to them!
What a purgative performance.
'Twould make people Buddhistic,
And do away with the wars.
You'd have a better opinion of life
For the stench. Nothing like strong youth,

Strong love, strong corpses boiling,
Quick with effervescence.
And hang on their heaving breasts
The jewels of women. They'll sink
Down slowly in the fleshly mess,
And at the last shine on and dazzle the earth.
An acute eye will pluck the glory
Of their indestructibility.
Page Hieronymus Bosch.

JOHN

You betray yourself, fellow,
And in the name of frivolity
Entertain us with a quite serious notion.
I glimpse even a spiritual
Regenerative principle
In your suggested and unlikely tactic.
But you employ a symbol for your
Metaphysics; otherwise they would vanish.
They would go back to the blood
And become the simple energy of action.
There is no necessity to change
The various burial rites of the world;
They are forms of human decency.
You would do better to apply your fancy
To the living,
Who stand in need of vitalizing notions.

PERCY

Have at you. I am Air-engine.
And incandescence is the sole sweet of the world.

JOHN

You are in danger of becoming a theolog an.
If you would put your views
Into a somewhat less heretical mould,
Even encase them in a cloak

Foreign to their character,
You might get a Rockefeller fellowship,
And study a year at Rio.
But you are only man after all,
The actor-animal.

PRISCILLA

Well, apparently I am here
Only as an objective symbol of
Your opinion of women:
I must suffer your talk.
You are always dissatisfied;
Fomenting ideas
As if the world could be changed.

PERCY

There's no more happiness in the world
Than a squirrel has with a nut.
You crack it open, eat it up,
And want more. But ideas
Are everywhere in the sky.
Come, fly by whimsicality.

JOHN

You ought to work for the City Company.
You could wear spikes,
Climb up poles like your ancestors,
And thereby carry electricity to the people.
If you were less ubiquitous and more single
I would want to cope with you.
Come, let me put some salt on your tail.
Your shallowness—

PERCY

Shallow? Then air is shallow,
Through which we see to heaven.

Shallow? Then water is shallow,
Of which we are all composed.
Shallow? Then morning's atmosphere,
Lakes, rivers, rills and streams
Are shallow. What is your jealous depth
But layers and layers of shallows? What
Profundity, but a schoolmaster's
Multiplications of a feather falling.
Shallow? Then I'll lie down on the wee
Boat of a feather, and sail in the heavenly air.
I count on the docility
Of men to save them much trouble.
Here is an old one, a seller of papers,
Bearing his load of defunct news
Homeward in the centre of night.
Life makes him
Faithful to his duty. He says
Good-night gently, when you pass.
And I daresay he is as good as
Your schizophrenetic synthetic dictators.
Shallow? Come praise whimsicality.

PRISCILLA

I say, do you mind, I must be leaving——

JOHN

Why, I'm awfully sorry, won't you——

PRISCILLA

Good-bye——

JOHN

You've driven the lovely creature off
With your frail bombast.

77

I must go. This is not what I was.
This is something else. This is pure Phoenix.
Come feel it. No, you can't. For though
You were vampire and drank my blood,
You would not get me. Fetch me
The past in a basket lined with grass,
If you think to. Bring me
A bucket full of huckleberries
Plucked at ten years old, if you will.
Present me my first virgin,
If you can. Or dig up my bones
When I shall have been a decade dead,
If you are able. No, no,
I am something else than I am.
I am the tickings of clocks whose ratchets
Wear away now in the mill stream.
And the rust of them, standing in old barns.
I am the bud of the leaf
Whose remains stick on my heels . . .
Oh, I am the lad's eyes,
When there was wonder upon them
Like flax twinkling in the wind and sun . . .
The same skull; Plato and Aristotle,
Plus Shakespeare, and Donne, and Blake, and Marx,
And as gone as old Neanderthal.

JOHN

Would you mind coming along?

PERCY

Oh, that's all right, but the world's
Nothing but a pile of filth. The
Relations between men are as excellent as hell,
They are all well ordered and arranged beforehand.
There's nothing so full of end-results

As friendship; and nothing so crafty
As men in love with mountains.
When you have gone through all,
Evil stares you in the strict, emaciated face.
But you're not emancipated yet.
You can no more conquer yourself
Than walk on Pluto. The good falls
Into a big disrespect and a dusty bin;
Evil flowers out incandescent,
Ready to burn you up again.
The masters of life have as much
Energy as it; the rest fade off.

JOHN

I say, do you mind coming along?

PERCY

There are those who say flowers
Have no more to say; look there,
There is the world pure and final,
Nothing else to it. There are those
Who say those are partial fellows,
Befriended by lenses. These are troubled
By a fire in the guts and say
Microscopes do no good.
The messy little bluet is only
A sallying forth of some knotted ganglia.
They have a great room between the ears,
Wherein they play games. There are others,
Who can hardly tell whether they are
In Venice or Canton, but they are
Sure neither has the importance of a thumb tack.
They doubt they doubt their own doubts,
And end where they began—a right
Doleful dingle-dangle state indeed.
The experimenters are, sooth-la,

79

The only realizers. That is
Because they refuse to think.
They put chemicals in test tubes,
Measure the results, and have no
Astonishment whatever at the conflagration.
But the artist saves the world.
I have been everywhere, done everything.
There is nothing left but
To search out the bosom of God,
The chief receding pleasure known to man.

The searching is ever better
Than the finding; when you have found something
You must keep it, which is another kind of searching.
If you search for an unknown woman,
You must always be seeking. If you
Marry one, you must, though you have her by you,
Seek out new ways continually to appease her.
Get a child, and you go back to God.

JOHN

Well, come along now, Percy.

PERCY

I have come to no conclusion.

JOHN

You have come to no conclusion.

PERCY–JOHN

We have come to no conclusion.

PERCY

Conclusion is too inclusive.
To(o) crude warfare my food is air.

80

ODE TO THE CHINESE PAPER SNAKE

I

Held on the slightest of bamboo poles,
Suspended from the most voluble of delicate strings,
Heavy in the head, as is proper to subtelty,

His limitation is his slyest and activist, most charm;
Achieves with the least energy the greatest purpose;
Frail in the body, liable to tear, a dissolute.

His eye is horny, he has the feather of imagination
For a fang; his hiss is what you are.
The circuitous pleases him most: circles are endless.

II

The father of a metaphysical principle,
Made in Hong Kong but sold in San Francisco,
The paper snake is foreign to the people of Maine
And has never been seen in the hives of Vienna.

Nearest to stillness his force is most potent.
Thus he adumbrates the meaning of innocence,
Liable in gross action to the unsalvageable and comic;
His least motions manipulate the fiercest evil.

Delicacy is also the mark of civilization
And this is a most uncultured Satanism;
Him no Spengler fingered into exotic play,
Nor divested him of his striking parody.

III

As sex he would be simple, but nothing is simple,
So sexually he bares the fascination of centuries.
He triumphs adept, formally, evident, exquisite.

The ultimate investing philosopher of the future,
A paper snake gives way to none in egoism.
His confidence is masterful and ritualistic,

His is the innate totality of knowledge.
A pertness poses his profundity, deftly expressed,
And it has in it the guile and the smile of the sly.

IV

The pleasantest and the most profound trickery
Is that you can handle as you will this apostle.
It is you who think you control the principle of evil,
It is you who think you invite the charming play of the good.

Nor should we forget forgetfulness, which he induces;
Such rite of resolution is another of his provinces.
Neither Chinese nor Christian, his characteristic of universality

Intrigues as blood, as intellect, as purity, as impurity;
Most inanimate the Chinese snake becomes most animate
Seemingly in the very laughter and sorrow of your being.

V

Aeschylus should have asked of this plaything an answer
As Sophocles spent a lifetime in honouring him;
He was too inward for the Western tone of Shakespeare;
Baudelaire knew him in Paris as a cat.

The heaviness in the Hebrews did not see his dandyism.
Perhaps the greatest effrontery to knowledge
Is that you can manipulate your own fate

And as I dandle this fragile, motionable creature
His invitation is the subtle invitation of evil,
The prospect of the Immortal in a paper toy.

VI

And as I think of his perfect, immaterial existence
I am reminded of the deepest human sympathies,
While in his coyness I can make him run.
Inventiveness is his saucy mode, as he spins.

Delectable is the passionate language of the snake,
His motion has in it the stillness of all delectation,
Ancient the sinuousness, instructive the sensibility

For death is in the imagination of that tongue;
But the poison you create in entertaining him
Is swallowed up in waves of orgiastic love.

VII

Or maybe as music as an aftermath
The tantalizing poise always about to be destroyed,
Vagaries of the vigorous, quagmires of the pellucid,
Indices of the contaminations of the realities

You will perceive in fabulous sounds this serpent.
He is present to your skull as in a mirror,
It is the music of your blood you see in his visage.

Delightful is the persuasion of this destroyer,
He is the charming absolute of crumbling fingers,
The dancer, the actor fabulous in the abstract.

VIII

Self-knowledge is the tempter on the stick,
Fair is his eye, ineradicable his logic,
Unquestionable his intention to destroy,
Perdurable his ability to maintain!

For you have coiled him up upon himself,
You have looked him in his evil eye,
Adroit, you spurned him into fantasy,

And you are the pattern of his prophecy!
You are the structure of his massive eye,
And you increase his inviolability.

BURR OAKS

THE JUNGLE

It is in the jungle one finds the secret springs.
Spiny nature there, in thickets uncontestable
Coils her secrets and makes pure her spiritings.
From the opulence of the burdock the heart sings.
From the mystery of the grapevines and the plum trees
The soul will struggle to be free, inextricably
Bent in the human gaze and warmth of blood
To the folded fragrance of the ground beneath.
In the freedom of their fastness squirrels play.
It is odd, at his unaccustomed level, to look a rabbit in
The eye, beneath a tree: who is the hypnotizer, you, or he?
The fear of the thicket is what you see.
Fear will keep you from the remotest dens
Of the snakes, but will lead you to find them.
The birds by favouring denseness are contrived
To viewless melody twice their size.
The skin stings and smarts with all surprise.
The jungle, vigorous, various, interminably
Changeless, is never grown to, a foreign fastness.
You cannot see up through to the latticed sky.
To its secret strength you return again,
A mysterious place unspoiled by man,
In which you can be endlessly listening
To wildness in the weeds, the intoxicants of things.

THE ATTIC

The attic and the cedar closet—nostalgia!
Who has not dreamed evasive dreams
In the strange disorder of the attic trunks and boxes,
Fantastic clothes, broken dolls, grandfather's canes?
And in that world of broken strangeness
Had glimpses of the profound aberration of the world?
And crept in among mother's old rustling dresses
Overpowered by the cedar ether from the cedar trees?
While from the high tight windows, surveying the vast
World of trees, grove, river and pasture
It was a citadel never the world would cure,
Nor all its years of struggle, philosophy, or knowledge
Divest of a delirium of strange charm.
A special place is the attic where one goes
For special purposes, where anarchy reigns,
Oddness is the prince of disinheritance,
Angularity expresses the confusion of the senses,
Time is suicidally overcome and diverted,
Chaos is come without pain of reality.
O who has not loved hours among attic things?
Who has not grieved to return to the world downstairs?

THE GROVE

The grove is a stately place, calm and free,
Wherein the immane sky looks vastly down
On health and ease: the trees measure world's
Harmony. I have sat with my back against them
All a summer's afternoon, and shucked the big acorns.
The lawn is smooth and pleased; each grass blade
Beneath the protection of the strong burr oaks.
This is a world should never end.
It is a world controlled by men,
The trees placed for their healthful ease,
Which give the shade of happy years.
Security comes from the massive trunks and branches,

85

A lightness of heart from the luxuriance of the leaves.
Here the play of the imagination without curb
Combines sky and earth in knitted sanctity.
Abated would seem to be nature's processes
That the soul sing only as of holiday.
Death is nowhere to be seen in the grove,
Time has not sullied the delicate encryption
Of a forked hoof in the ground, Pan's love?
While here no sinister storms or fears
Trouble the mind with sin or tears.
O the grove, so large, so hale, so comfortable
Holds a deep music pure and noble.
Shall we not sit here always in pleasure and ease,
Beneath the rugged strength of the burr oak trees?

THE ORCHARD

It is in the orchard where a symbol flourishes.
An orchard of apple trees, mountainous white and pink in
     Spring!
Where mothers hold their small children up in the branches,
Little knowing the death time has in store for them.
I see the Maypole still, the gay dresses and the picnics,
The joyous rounds of innocent play and laughter.
How far away that vision of unparalleled splendour!
Unattainable the glowing of effulgence of the balmy scene!
Yet though all turn to worm and dust, to death and ashes,
The springtide of the rich orchard returns anew,
The fullness of the blossoms, a trust and a returning,
Fullness and solace of man against his loss,
O the glory of the orchard trees in their full bloom
And the memory of their scent keen as the skin of love,
The apple blossoms in full bloom before the apple comes.
Let it be kept as if somehow eternal and true,
Let it be believed when belief can be believed,
Against the worm in the flower, the cancer in the lung.
Let the mind hold its delicate balance of belief,

The glory come again in the memory:
Time ruined the perfection with unattainability,
Underground are the loved blossoms, the lovely ones.

THE BARN

In the barn you know the large soft cows
And they are your own best friends, even.
Their mild eyes are meant to teach constancy
To your impetuous and erratic restlessness.
If acceptance after the storms of decades
Is the ounce of wisdom in electrified flesh,
Philosophy can end in the eye of a cow.
The eye of a cow is a picture of sufferance.
The whole attitude of the animal is gentle.
It has learned the lesson of the pacifist
And by not fighting back has not been destroyed:
Even has rewarded its captor with bright drink,
A kindness never learned spiritually by man.
Deep in the obscure brain of this mild beast
Is knowledge of the opulence of mother earth.

Upon the skies of loftiest imagination man can gaze,
In no wise control the purpose and movement of the stars.
Let him then in the confines of human pastures
And upon the heart of man graze with some study
Learning from the cow the nourishment of those acres,
Supported by the supporting love of fellows.
I tossed old Daisy an extra toss of hay
When I thought of these things that early day.
Twenty years later I have thought it over
And still admire an attitude of clover.

THE PASTURE

The pasture is a field of changing vision.
Seen from a height, it stretches to distant woods.
On either side the Cedar River flows
From Baudler's swimming hole to the old sand bank.

The distant river is enchantment still,
Its least and living turn and intimacy.
In Spring it is adventure's steadfastness,
With bogs and flags; with eggs and hatched birds found;
With gophers snared in strings in deftest summer;
With list of seeds of the milkweed pod in drifting fall;
With banks of dangerous winter snowstorm snowfall.
An estate not incomprehensible, but mapped
With every zest between the barbed wire fences.
Year in, year out, the pasture is to lie in
And gaze at intellect within the sky,
And gaze through intellect to spirituality.
It is the same earth at death you will lie in,
Old earth pressing up against your new thigh,
Ancient grasses at the corner of your eye,
Air that incorporates your flesh in sky
While quite beyond the reach of men
Everywhere are treasures of profundity—
That forty years will pass away, or more,
With nothing learned in action not sensed in the earth,
In silent acts of adoration,
Prone in the pasture grass.

THE CEMETERY

To sit by graves of freshest green, and watch
The robins pass, beneath ephermerid clouds,
For long hours silent, that is the breathless ease
Of searching a high mystery,
And to be quite out of mind with ecstasy
Realizing the shortness of your stay,
The voluptuous benefit of rosy day,
And humbly to accept primordial constancy,
Your death, total decay,
Obliteration to so serene a sky
As touches now your cheek, and now your eye,
With such a fine delay
That it makes you say,

I,
Beyond the greenness of my youth and ease,
Lying by a grave under the trees
Fully conscious of my state,
Aware of the whole fate,
Accept the blue tenure of the sky,
Time's vanishing point in me,
Then young, or old,
When world's no more to see,
Let worms have deep their play
As men had their deep strife,
Let the day be other
And let

Come what may.

DAM NECK, VIRGINIA

Anti-aircraft seen from a certain distance
On a steely blue night say a mile away
Flowers on the air absolutely dream-like,
The vision has no relation to the reality.

The floating balls of light are tossed easily
And float out into space without a care,
They the sailors of the gentlest parabolas
In a companionship and with a kind of stare.

They are a controlled kind of falling stars,
But not falling, rising and floating and going out,
Teaming together in efflorescent spectacle
Seemingly better than nature's: man is on the lookout.

The men are firing tracers, practising at night.
Each specialist himself precision's instrument,
These expert prestidigitators press the luminence
In knowledge of and ignorance of their doing.

They do not know the dream-like vision ascending
In me, one mile away: they had not thought of that.
Huddled in darkness behind their bright projectors
They are the scientists of the skill to kill.

As this sight and show is gentle and false,
The truth of guns is fierce that aims at death.
Of war in the animal sinews let us speak not,
But of the beautiful disrelation of the spiritual.

THE FURY OF AERIAL BOMBARDMENT

You would think the fury of aerial bombardment
Would rouse God to relent; the infinite spaces
Are still silent. He looks on shock-pried faces.
History, even, does not know what is meant.

You would feel that after so many centuries
God would give man to repent; yet he can kill
As Cain could, but with multitudinous will,
No farther advanced than in his ancient furies.

Was man made stupid to see his own stupidity?
Is God by definition indifferent, beyond us all?
Is the eternal truth man's fighting soul
Wherein the Beast ravens in its own avidity?

Of Van Wettering I speak, and Averill,
Names on a list, whose faces I do not recall
But they are gone to early death, who late in school
Distinguished the belt feed lever from the belt holding pawl.

AN AIRMAN CONSIDERS HIS POWER

I was in the days of peace
Of warlike tissues made,
And that was a strange man
Fighting in a shade.

All things by opposites go,
Truth has there his lease,
Peace has come with war,
War that came with peace.

It is events that make us peer.
But you will veer some way, no doubt,
In balance by your natural aptitude,
My proposition quite thrown out.

Yet I know in the bomb's release
The truth I felt of the will,
From destruction is peace,
In peace the will to kill.

AT THE END OF WAR

God, awful and powerful beyond the sky's acre,
Lord God who looks down upon fighting men,
Who sees the bloody folly of them and their wickedness,
The Admiral with his cap and the private with his can,
The aviator shrouded in goggles and the marine bayoneted,
The men in the bureaus mating rubber stamps, carbonizing
    history,
The poets raving in their uncontestable ravening
The war poets who were ever at war
Before the wars, and after the wars,

Forgive them, that all they do is fight
In blindness and fury,

Forgive them for passion, and animality
Like a cloud vitiating their members,
Forgive mankind for its abominable stupidity
And fury of action,
And men for the misuse of their intelligence,
And for the intelligence that must ever be misused,
For the impenetrable fierceness you have put into them.

And may their guts justly come to rot,
The Admiral, the private
The aviator and the bayoneted or garrotted,
In bureaus the silhouetted
In pages the gavotted
Or the hooded eagles

May they all be established in the grace of time
Far away from the scenes of their crime,
Their bones awash on Himavat
Or their flesh blown apart in the air,
Translated from the terrible mummery of humanity
Into the translucence of Thy care
And done with passion, ego gone,
Self-deceiving deceased,
The unforgivability
Unpretendable,
Protect him in the pain of his erroneous breath,
Bring him to account,
Bring him to judgment,
Let the show be over and the yelling quieted.

Then, Lord God Almighty,
Visit upon mankind Thy terrible wrath
Merciless in the great eye of Thy mercy,
Altogether annihilate him, in hell,
Or in the dust of eternal nothingness,
But be Thou his condemner,

Take his life who gave it to him,
Destroy him,
Bring to an end imperfection,
And to an end his eternal frivolity.

(His passions shall be minimized
And his wars seem a dark blot
And he shall suffer plenitude
With the resurgence of the grain)

For they cannot think straight, or remember what they said,
Cannot keep their word,
Or realize how soon they will be dead,
Nor distinguish between verities
Who lust over presences,
Nor be faithful
Who are wrathful,
Nor escape animal passion
With cross-bow, slit-trench, Napalm bomb, atom bomb.

For shadows punish them when they are bright
And pride ruins them when they are strong
And time is the just instrument
That sweeps the seaman and the Admiral along,
May they never escape Thy wrath,

May they be woken up, blasted late,
Or reduced to eternal silences,
But may, pray God Almighty,
Man the cocky fighter,
The stupid and the self-destroyer,
The selfish and the vain,
The harmful cheater
The malicious debater,
The incurable self-lover
And the boring warrior,
The simpleton killer

May he learn humility
May humility be insinuated
More subtly than evil
Which brought ruin rocking him

May he turn the other cheek
Not bitten yet by worm of hate
May joy be his abandonment
In Thy forgiveness early and late

And may he learn not to fight
And never to kill, but love,
Never, never to kill, but love,
May he see Thy holy light.

A CEREMONY BY THE SEA

Unbelievable as an antique ritual,
With touch of Salamis and Marathon,
Through what visions of rebirth and death
At Atlantic's blue, hot, and sparkling edge—

War's head is up, war's bloody head,—
The thirtieth of May beats through America
With here the band, the boardwalk, and the speeches
Masking with blaze the parted beach crowds.

The traffic still restless, the loudspeaker proud,
Young couples in swimsuits strolling hand in hand
Beyond the crowd, self-interested, not attending.
But comes a hush like shimmer of summer over all,

With solemn tones the names are called, John Pettingill,
Roger Ashcroft, Timothy O'Shaughnessy, Patrick
O'Shaughnessy, Olaf Erickson, Alan Hieronymus,
William Henry Cabe, Neil Campbell, Victor Giampetruzzi. . . .

Long pause after each name, as mother or father,
Grandfather or grandmother, uncle, or brother
Awkwardly walks through the entangling sand
With sheaf or wreath of flowers to the flower-waggon,

Burgeoning with brightness beneath the bandstand.
The newly dead! The young, the dead far away,
In the strange young reality of their war deaths
Too young for this austere memorial.

The last name is called, the last flower is funded,
As people stand in the daze of the actual,
Then eight young men of the Army and Navy,
Almost naked, strong swimmers of the tides of life,

Their muscles blending in among the flowers,
Take up, four each, the flower-twined ropes.
Like a mad disturbance, hafts to the hilt of earth air,
Eighty Corsairs plummet out of the sky

From high inland down over the bandstand,
Four abreast, flash out over the sand
Over the ocean, and up easily and turn.
The deafening noise and closeness is a spell.

Then the flower waggon by the stalwart ones slowly
Through the crowd begins to go to the sea,
And as it draws, the ocean opens up its heart
To the heavy hearts of mourners by the sea's edge.

These, all kinds and conditions of men,
Thereafter follow across that bright, that transient course
As they would pay their tribute to the waves,
To the justice unaccountable of final things,

Followers of flowers; the gorgeous waggon-coffin
Drawing the blood out of the crowd, slow-passing it.

And lastly I saw an aged Italian couple
Too old to stumble through that catching sand,

The backs of their bodies bent like man himself,
Ancient as Marathon or as Salamis,
New and ancient as is America,
Diminish with laborious march toward the water.

From the platform funereal music played
In dirge that broke upon purged air
While now in mid distance, far by the shore, the new fated
Stood; then the powerful, the graceful youths

Like gods who would waft to far horizons
Drew the waggon in, which then a boat of flowers
They swam with, dim swan on the searoad.
A waiting gunboat fired a last salute.

WORLD WAR

Flutesong willow winding weather,
Tomorrow lovely undulant today,
Glorious bird glide in forest glade,
In meadow golden lissom girl dance,

Tremble air with never yesterday,
Grassy twirling boyfoot triumphing,
Budding bough drops lovely lording,
Pearling cuckoobrook cool ecstasy,

Woven from lucid sunny nest,
World of mellow willow mist,
Now forever pleasures piping,
Honey supple body wonderful:

Strike down, batter! shatter! splinter!
Destroy! fracture! cripple! butcher!

Knock! beat! whack! cuff!
Ruin! gash! smash! blast!

Baby Red Breasted Chained Nippled,
Pavement Clattering People Crippled,
Youth Courageous Finger Felled,
Nutty Manhood Maggot Shelled,

Buzzards Smiling Char the Sky,
Pain Caressing Bites the Eye,
Grass Has Adders Time Vipers,
The Heart Burns its Lifted Ladders,

Howls the Whirlwind Over the World,
Tempests Quaking Shake the World,
The Earthquake Opens Abrupt the World,
Cold Dreadful Mass Destruction.

BROTHERHOOD OF MEN

I

Caught there, then, on the Rock. At Corregidor
Caged with the enemy, sleepless in inexactness
The mind wavering with wishes of decisions,
Fear frequented the bowels in their fury,
Actor I was, avid of answers, egress,
Hungry there in a hovel, had to steal food,
Harry inventiveness, deft of devices.
Had to creep by the inching invaders
Lifting my life in my hands, lily-livered,
With motive of man's ancient menace
Dared danger, gave to a dying friend.
Often eased the enemy, agile of acquiescence,
Stole drugs from the cupboard, mates to maintain.
Saw tortures, and tall tales expedited,
Urged the underground, close escapes lived with.

97

Lined up with the blistered, the intrepid,
Passive at bayonet point in the belly.
Flinched not, was cast down with the feckless,
Pretender on purpose, mastering machination.
Thought of home and youth as sickness prevailed,
The shining sitters at stately banquets,
Lofty in lapsing dreams as dooms eventuated,
Blind in trust, wondered forever of survival,
Cupped heads in my hands at baleful midnights,
Waxed wary only companions to save,
Thought nothing of self, nightmares of dyings.
Bones softened by black malnutrition,
Bloated were heads and legs ulcerous,
Never gave in to the enemy, found fierce
Store in physical love for dying brothers,
Wondered on wakening how I survived oft
With strength to stall the staggering.
Played opossum to the enemy's piercing examinations,
Smile saintly, collaborated clearly,
Never gave in to the enemy, death was common.
Came ruthless purgation of the pale living,
Undreamed of excruciations, excrement of prison,
Diseased men doled on the death march of Bataan.
Fatigue was early, fierce was the fury,
Blazed by bayonets side-fellows fell,
Stumbled stalwarts, cursed many,
Crazy became some in the heat of hatred,
Infernal the features of famished men,
The enemy edged us in, egged us on.
Violence of life in the vividness of madness,
Kept by miracle of man's sufferance
Some semblance of order, reduction to essence,
First blanch of weakness was first broached.
Down to the doom of man's mastery of self,
Fate was fearful, fate dandled the balance.
Strong those seemed who cracked first, cried,
Crumbled in clairvoyance to butt-stroke of rifle.

98

Miles were nightmares, water was absent,
Mercy was nowhere, but stood the gaff,
Wonder of wonders, never knew how.
Hardest was not to move muscle
When friends were violated; vicious visitations
And violent strokes ebbed the naked strength.
Eyes should not see such sanguine spectacle,
Death not dare such darting depravity.
Retaliators were whipped, naked were whacked,
Were cuffed quailing, pierced with pikes.
Soonest were doomed those who cared aught,
Care for others in the carking tribulation.
Kept as if eventless, played against the enemy,
Looked not sidewise, helped not the helpless;
Cunning of the canny bred continuance.
Survived the death march; men are makeshift,
Weary of wishes to kill every one, weary
The enemy of watching comedy of twitches.
Favored by nature were the wan survivors.

II

Came lassitude and despair of the mind,
Mounted months of weakness, filth of fellows,
Pain of realization, poison of water.
Death was daisy, the mind followed fictions,
Spirit was luckless, lack of news told.
Emaciation was the flag of emancipation
Death waved at the doors always closed.
And then was transferred to Cabanatuan.
Sweaty and reckless, but holding to truth
Thought of turn of the nightmare tide,
Was able to steal in the stalking midnights,
Gave grace of grain to lads groaning,
Maggots were many, relished with rice,
Bitterness of necessity, better nourishment.
And thought of home hale in the States,

99

Impossible presentiments of feverish dreams,
Kept with all incommunicable dreams,
Vast vistas of times impossible.
Heard months later of fates foregone,
Heard the curt shots of ones caught.
Mentally deranged were many, no mail came.
Enemy was endless, workers were listless,
The down were soon out, the dead were left days.
Turned at night to clasp your friend dying,
Shielded him; woke clasping a death's head.

Monsters were moving; sickness established,
Endurance was endless, never was mercy.
Were mild, many, with infection, lips were livid,
Heads swelled like cabbages before the soft death-rattle.
Came day of dispatch, was chosen with others,
Knew nothing, but was sailing by ship.
Rumors ran, shipment of prisoners to Japan.
The heart lifted somewhat, but dazed was desire,
Man suffering much cannot believe early.
Little knew those of the perils impending.
Haggard by hundreds, thrown into the hold,
Heat staggered the stifling; time wore on
As we wavered in the knowledge of the water,
Packed like pigs, herded in jeopardy,
Mass and mess of mankind standing up,
Heat harried us, parched were people,
Panic mounted in pandemonium,
Merciless was the murderous sun, murderous
The enemy with machine-guns at the hold's top.
Days unendurable, the dead fallen were trampled.
In desperation, doughty, doomed countrymen
Climbed on others, climbed the hot iron ladder,
At top were shot down, fell on their fellows.
So close were packed all was a clenching,
Madness was manifest, infernal the struggle,
Urine was drunk by many, rampant was chaos,

Came wild men at each other, held off attackers,
Some slit the throats of the dead,
Drank the blood outright, howled wailing,
Slit the wrists of the living, others
With knives, or with fangs ravenous,
I saw them drinking the blood of victims,
Hell I was in, this was immitigible Hell.
Endless hours fought off famished, crazed attackers.
Savage the senses in dreams of delirium,
Never knew how I surrendered not,
Saw clearly my mother in the midst of terror:
'Persevere. Persevere. Persevere. Persevere.'
Faith beyond reason, wrecked beyond words,
I dogged clung, daft before danger,
Dazed by disaster, damned in the hold.
And hung on God knows how, saved by my nature.
Some peculiarity of nature saved me, hundreds perished.
Would never have won, but our own planes
Came hungry, hunting enemy ships.
Knew not our own men were therein.
Bomb blast in the hold next killed all there,
We were as if raised out of water.
Clambered to deck tottering and reckless,
Gone were victors, machine-guns vacated,
Like bales of lumber dead were stacked on the decks.
Caught handfulls of sugar from wrenched sacks,
Stuffed mouth, pockets; jumped over, water revived me,
Saw the shore and swam to save me.
Some seventy swam, of all holds' hundreds.
Crept to a clearing, fraternity of survivors.
The enemy entered the clearing, commanded us.
A marine's leg was shattered, smoked calmly
One cigarette discovered; clasp-knife severed his leg.
(Heroes were many). He died gamely.

A summed spectacle in the sultry sunlight
Our sapped band was, after hellish onslaught.

We stiffened our resources, bonds were breakless.
Speechless were the depths of humanity,
We were the living, no time for understanding.
Again the enemy did not kill us,
Ammunition doubtless sparse on this island.
But took our shoes, practically fatal,
None could hope to escape without them
And live long in the barbed jungles;
Soon would be forfeit to tortures of thorns.
Weakness persisted, rest was undertaken,
Watery rice with maggots always our ration.
Now numbness of spirit prevailed, what more
Could happen? How long could man endure
Unknowable fate? A ship came to take us,
This time without torture we got to Japan.

III

My mind was heavy and my luck was dark,
From chaos I came, to greater chaos went,
Stubborn of spirit, subtle suborner,
Four years in prisons and vile execrations
I endured, and worked to save my companions.
Fame I never had at home among fellows, was never
Known as the bright who knew where he was going,
Suffered severely from cul-de-sac sensations,
But I had animal cunning, abundantly,
Reserves I had that were boundless, idiot cunning.
I did better, being instinct with the basic,
Undeluded of delusions, had knowledge of nature,
Queerness quested my queerness, madness not maimed me,
Basilisk my eye baleful to baneful totality,
Delicate my decisions due to no dearth of nature,
But to strangeness I gave ever strange nurture.
The normal, those with notions pre-conceived,
Died early, or died late, but always died.
To test them so far nature never intended,

It took madness to fight madness, savage simplicity
To slay savagery, sleights of mind for savagery,
Tricks of balance and tenacious trickery.
Fared lax like one in the forfeited herd,
Yet undefinable nature used my example yearly.
I, weak, had strength beyond the strongest,
Wounds I wore out, amazing to myself.
Held, helpless, to the help of Heaven,
Expected death at every ditch,
Only hope was the help of helping others.
I observed those survived best were feminine,
Fared on duplicity, dark deceivers;
Most male were most manhandled, maimed.
Womanish men were puckish, pictures of Psyche.
The enemy sensed their lack of enmity,
Entered they had into subtle sympathy,
Fragile balances saved them savage bayonets.

Winter came in heathenish hell-holes,
Water was wicked, cold was killing,
And never knew how the war was going.
Slept with diseased brothers to keep off the cold.
Low was language, life left us slowly,
Some sank into states of sodden trance,
Longing to lie in cold bed and to die,
Weary of spirit, would not wake, will-less.
Warmed the waning, months at a time,
In coughing nights of incurable cold,
Tempted to bend to the bed of death beckoning
Beyond disease's ravage, blessing of rest endless.
Peculiarity of nature nerved me nevertheless,
Locked in bunks befouled with bloating brothers,
I forced fellows to follow me, fall on the floor,
Get out of beds where they were breathing only,
And stand in dark days against compulsion of death.
Broken bones were left to brokenness,
Festering flesh was guest to feebleness.

Work was a wisdom and kept the mind alive,
Worked for nine months sewing buttonholes.
Long had forgotten of justice, but never
Of justicing; never gave in to the enemy,
Never surrendered, the enemy was myself.
Monthly made him think I loved him,
In some strange manner I loved my captor,
I belonged to mankind, all were responsible.
In his place would I not have done the same?
My bayonet would not have pierced the plucky,
Hatred would halt somewhere, heavy of heart.
We were only soldiers doing our duty,
All imprisoned in primal curses,
All commanded by evil in man's nature.
Learned in the longest years of my life,
In depths of dejection, disjunctive thralls,
Grains of good in the coldest killers,
Quest of kindness of the unbelievers,
Qualms of conscience, costliness of guilt.
Enormous it was, and frail were all,
Victim and victor alike vacillated.
Error was everywhere, ever flagellant,
Freakish the force of death or survival.
Each event and trial was unique,
No law held for all operations.
In gruelling slowness of gravid time
Never saw women, forgotten were children.

IV

Rumors of liberation. We could not believe it.
Liberation came. Planes came over parachuting
Packages. One plummeted through a sky-light,
Broke one of our legs. Greedy as children,
We ate chocolate until we were sick,
Suspect bellies could not stand it.
It would take us years to get well,

Our bones soft and easily breakable.
My hand broke, opening the door of a car.

Rings I have, watches, tokens, a dog tag
To take back to the land of the living,
From the dead to deliver to fathers or sisters,
Cherished possessions of my luckless companions
Lost in four years of rooted abuse.
O to forget, forget the fever and famine,
The fierceness of visions, the faith beyond reason,
To forget man's lot in the folly of man.
And swear never to kill a living being,
To live for love, the lost country of man's longing.

And yet I know (a knowledge unspeakable)
That we were at our peak when in the depths,
Lived close to life when cuffed by death,
Had visions of brotherhood when we were broken,
Learned compassion beyond the curse of passion,
And never in after years those left to live
Would treat with truth as in those savage times,
And sometimes wish that they had died
As did those many crying in their arms.

INDIAN PIPE

Searching once I found a flower
    By a sluggish stream.
Waxy white, a stealthy tower
    To an Indian's dream.
    This its life supreme.

Blood red winds the sallow creek
    Draining as it flows.
Left the flower all white and sleek,
    Fainting in repose.
    Gentler than a rose.

Red man's pipe is now a ghost
  Whispering to beware.
Hinting of the savage host
  Once that travelled there.
  Perfume frail as air.

'GO TO THE SHINE THAT'S ON A TREE'

Go to the shine that's on a tree
When dawn has laved with liquid light
With luminous light the nighted tree
And take that glory without fright.

Go to the song that's in a bird
When he has seen the glistening tree,
That glorious tree the bird has heard
Give praise for its felicity.

Then go to the earth and touch it keen,
Be tree and bird, be wide aware
Be wild aware of light unseen,
And unheard song along the air.

'SOMETIMES THE LONGING FOR DEATH'

Sometimes the longing for death,
Imaginative death, comes hard.
Not the unimaginable, last gasp,
But lift to supernatural love.

And sometimes death is achieved
In the visionary place of the mind,
New life, painful no more,
Where hope does not need to deter us.

Is it for this, most personal, most secure
Life turns, in goodness, and in evil
To tear our wits out of our wills
To its built, tremendous godhead?

AT NIGHT

In the dust are my father's beautiful hands,
In the dust are my mother's eyes.
Here by the shore of the ocean standing,
Watching: still I do not understand.

Love flows over me, around me,
Here at night by the sea, by the sovereign sea.

Gone is that bone-hoard of strength;
Gone her gentle motion laughing, walking.

Is it not strange that disease and death
Should rest, by the undulant sea?

And I stare, rich with gifts, alone,

Feeling from the sea those terrene presences,
My father's hands, my mother's eyes.

A LOVE POEM

I am the lightness that I know
And I am the terror that I seem;
The taint, the question, and the dream.
Perhaps you are also.

When the wind blows, and trees shake,
I think there is some comfort in them;
Else, in the silence of contemplation,
All harry me and my mind take.

Therefore, what I am interested in
Is the anatomy of time;
Whether there is anything substantial
In the world and flesh we are in.

But Love told me the answer,
In the moist garden, when the worms were out;
Love evaded the painful question,
When my eyes were a green dancer.

GOD AND MAN

My grandmother said I was an atheist
God said I was a man.
My father took me by the hand,
My mother vanished in a mist.

In the rich stores of the ether
The future was seen as the past,
Flesh was aerial prescience,
And the devil was seen last.

In time you have no grandmother
For ancient earth recedes.
Your father and your mother go,
But God says, you are a man.

Between budding leaf and blue sky
Angels of mercy were spreading,
Like bees around the cider-press
Diffusing this blood with murmurousness.

The angels were the archetypes.
Would go away while devils overcame
Time, and chased the crooked years,
You still lusting after evil.

Every one a father and a mother has
And every one more ancient staffs,
Yet all lose even loss itself
When God says, you are Man.

For man precedes his knowledge
Aroused within his variant myth,
A stalwart, fiery with animus
Whose death is only another dream.

And God has the deep justice,
And God has the last laugh.
To be God God needs man
As man needs God to be man.

THE HORSE CHESTNUT TREE

Boys in sporadic but tenacious droves
Come with sticks, as certainly as Autumn,
To assault the great horse chestnut tree.

There is a law governs their lawlessness.
Desire is in them for a shining amulet
And the best are those that are highest up.

They will not pick them easily from the ground.
With shrill arms they fling to the higher branches,
To hurry the work of nature for their pleasure.

I have seen them trooping down the street
Their pockets stuffed with chestnuts shucked, unshucked.
It is only evening keeps them from their wish.

Sometimes I run out in a kind of rage
To chase the boys away: I catch an arm,
Maybe, and laugh to think of being the lawgiver.

I was once such a young sprout myself
And fingered in my pocket the prize and trophy.
But still I moralize upon the day

And see that we, outlaws on God's property,
Fling out imagination beyond the skies,
Wishing a tangible good from the unknown.

And likewise death will drive us from the scene
With the great flowering world unbroken yet,
Which we held in idea, a little handful.

THE TOBACCONIST OF EIGHTH STREET

I saw a querulous old man, the tobacconist of Eighth Street.
Scales he had, and he would mix tobacco with his hands
And pour the fragrance in a paper bag.
You walked out selfishly upon the city.

Some ten years I watched him. Fields of Eire
Or of Arabia were in his voice. He strove to please.
The weights of age, of fear were in his eyes,
And on his neck time's cutting edge.

One year I crossed his door. Time had crossed before.
Collapse had come upon him, the collapse of affairs.
He was sick with revolution,
Crepitant with revelation.

And I went howling into the crooked streets,
Smashed with recognition: for him I flayed the air,
For him cried out, and sent a useless prayer
To the disjointed stones that were his only name:

Such insight is one's own death rattling past.

SEALS, TERNS, TIME

The seals at play off Western Isle
In the loose flowing of the summer tide
And burden of our strange estate—

Resting on the oar and lolling on the sea,
I saw their curious images,
Hypnotic, sympathetic eyes

As the deep elapses of the soul.
O ancient blood, O blurred kind forms
That rise and peer from elemental water:

I loll upon the oar, I think upon the day,
Drawn by strong, by the animal soft bonds
Back to a dim pre-history;

While off the point of Jagged Light
In hundreds, gracefully, the fork-tailed terns
Draw swift esprits across the sky.

Their aspirations dip in mine,
The quick order of their changing spirit,
More freedom than the eye can see.

Resting lightly on the oarlocks,
Pondering, and balanced on the sea,
A gauze and spindrift of the world,

I am in compulsion hid and thwarted,
Pulled back in the mammal water,
Enticed to the release of the sky.

THE CANCER CELLS

Today I saw a picture of the cancer cells,
Sinister shapes with menacing attitudes.
They had outgrown their test-tube and advanced,
Sinister shapes with menacing attitudes,
Into a world beyond, a virulent laughing gang.
They looked like art itself, like the artist's mind,
Powerful shaker, and the taker of new forms.
Some are revulsed to see these spiky shapes;
It is the world of the future too come to.
Nothing could be more vivid than their language,
Lethal, sparkling and irregular stars,
The murderous design of the universe,
The hectic dance of the passionate cancer cells.
O just phenomena to the calculating eye,
Originals of imagination. I flew
With them in a piled exuberance of time,
My own malignance in their racy, beautiful gestures
Quick and lean: and in their riot too
I saw the stance of the artist's make,
The fixed form in the massive fluxion.

I think Leonardo would have in his disinterest
Enjoyed them precisely with a sharp pencil.

FORMS OF THE HUMAN

I wanted to be more human
For I felt I thought too much
And for all the thinking I did—
More rabbits in the same hutch.

And how to be more human, I said?
I will tell you the way, I said.
I know how to do it, I said.
But what I said was not what I did.

I took an old garden hoe
And dug the earth, and planted there,
Not forgetting the compost too,
Three small beans that one might grow.

Three grew tall, but one was wild
So I cut off the other two,
And now I have a wild bean flower
The sweetest that ever grew.

OEDIPUS

Oedipus should have found exit from his dilemma:
Blinding of the eyes does not improve the insight.
How dark and magnificent were the Greeks! How
Their melancholy rings down the years to this day,

Rings in my ears the wail of the man going blind,
As universal blood streams through the firmament.
Not to unravel the doom but to accept it
Is even what I did when first I saw him bleeding.

Oedipus should have had a will to escape it.
He should have been able to outspan the plot.
Is there no perception to pierce through Fate?
Is nothing bright in man to dispel Destiny?

In barking and brittle light, in the antique air
I see him in the universal drench,
Fate that is stronger than the soul of man,
Destiny that rides us, whirlwind-like.

FRAGMENT OF NEW YORK, 1929

Four-thirty in the morning,
The coldest morning in late October.
Mechanical,

I stepped into clothes sprawled at hand before.
Effigies of tenuous waking dreams
Walked with me down the stairs,
Hardly realizations,—subtle separate sensations.
Chill air, and congealed skin,
So wake the mouth and hair.
I walked to work, Times Square
And all buildings little comprehended.
Unreality again, all this steel,
Height, lights: my feet alone know.
The usual stragglers pass. Stragglers?
Or only I? Or not I, they? Is
Nothing palatable but figs and coffee?
Then skirted along, briskly
Forty Second Street, to the west.
Head down, wind like a wire whip
Trying from neck to chest. Fingers
My collar closing are like a python's mouth.
My thighs feel good,
Action always feels good.
Except contemplation's,
When feet run in the brain.
Tenth Avenue, newspapers asleep in humble blankets.
Why look back? or even forward?
Feet can tell. Ten minutes late
This morning; see, night opens
One shade to the morning. The stars merely
Are pin points; not as on the Indian Ocean,
To be waked, naked, warm,
On a hatch, when stars sigh goodnight.
Not very wary. Eleventh Avenue,
I came around the corner and there,
Above the seven box-like and lamp-lit
Shelves of the packing house,
Glared the visitant metallic moon,
Canny as a dead man's eye.
Taormina. God, floods of foam.

There's a plumber playing pipes in my guts,
It screeches. Escapeless, common feeling.
Vapour from the factory rose up
Against the cold and paling light,
But vanished lower than the moon's aura.
Why must it be thus with you, never
To find the one untormented integer.
Surprise moon, four-thirty moon,
Dead moon, so rich with our ecstasies.
My stomach's got the goose flesh: wind of thin whips.
Into Hell again. I'll one glance,
Two glance, let it go, slip the moon's pierce,
Or grow great with old ravage.

Until the din became immense and profound,
A living horror of common death,
Merciless, disjunctive, co-ordinate;
Until relativity made this equable, and
Rhythm was levelled with it, it had
No meaning but simple action, happening.
Only one in a hundred kicked;
Kicked violently, pathos-maker,
Leer-long, with every energy.
A hog became a living curve,
Drew itself convex, from the vertical
Imposition of the ankle shackle.
Everything in nature curves.
So with beauty also; but I never
Decided; or decided so many times,
I have no decision. Decisions
Are practical, they do not increase the soul.
The killer's face! He is baffled now,
Seems. Moment. He poises
The tip of the knife at the throat.
So little is life. He cannot make
The one swift entry and up-jab.
Curious copulation, death-impregnation.

How the blood flows out
Dark red in a full stream;
Or some hold theirs in, muscles so tense,
One minute, then bewildered they rush into panic,
Six or eight or maybe only four
Wild screams, or grunts that can't
Get through the blood. This one baffles:
Odd. The vibrating free leg's too quick
For the killer to catch it. Then,
With almost a solemn decision,
The life-taker jams the terrified animal
On to a side rail: three more wait, with
Din-horrific screeches. They are dispatched
With able, easy gesture,
Purposive intercourse!
When there is a pause in the chain,
His inevitable great hand swings round
(Belly to belly) the daring pig.
Still its agony increases,
So much vitality expended,
Every muscle expresses itself
Against imminent death.
A dramatic instant of pause.
Of course there is no hope. In
Some dark way I wish
Life were less terrible.
These are all people strung up,
You understand. Not one chance,
Not a single.
Nature wants no virginity:
Must wed and be dead.
Big purpose (pig purpose) is to be killed.
We hope the inevitable hand
(Splendid huge veins there, bright wet
Red to the elbow) will be stayed
From him, from us. What a magic instant,
The tip at the throat, a little jab

Into the skin unfelt, then the
Deft probe, the jugular, conception.
Thus! And the admirable God's creature
Dies powerfully screaming.
A show! A show!
Come see the big Negro stick pigs.
That one was rare, to kick against the pricks.
His enthusiasm was unwarranted,
As if he were not of his genus,
But had the life of genius.

This is a vast sadistic enterprise.
Good for us, times, to see and feel
Down into sixty men. They
Stand upon greasy benches, with sharp knives.
The endless chain is begun,
With guttural as-if-eating-bolts groaning.
It is the endless chain of their labour.
Chilled hogs appear at the end
(As in a Blake angels would
At 'per me si va tra la perduta gente').
What if they, too, were people,
Some other intelligence were using,
As are used, these carcases.
The earlier initiation,
Neophytes knowing their Achilles heel,
Their tragic flaw, heads downward to earth,
Great Mother! All dead by
Some Pig Intelligence butchering.
Guts ripped out, young women too,
Old men, after fresh bath in a hot tank
Scalding the hair off. Then the
Whole family, and cousins Kate, Bertha, Percy,
Strung up, as I said, by Achilles
His heel. Ripped down
From penis, or vagina, through navel
(Inside out) to chin or cancer of the throat.

Faces sliced off, see fantastic mirth,
Comedy of errors, tragedy of desires,
On expressions so quick-changing.
Intestines on moving tables,
The last humiliation of having
The insides examined. If foul,
Condemned. Skinned, fat cut off,
Around we go on the chain slow,
And a great knife down, once, through the spine;
The skull split open, brains given an airing,
At last. Pea-sized pituitary.
I said the chilled hogs appeared at the far end,
A Negro big as Amazon,
Amazing, cuts them down onto the belt.
A white man, next him, like a giant
Marionette, with titan thews and blows,
(Conditioned by recurring necessity)
Chops with one vast climax
Belly from loin. His body
Turns, shifts, turns, swerves,
The splendid toy,
Man full-strong and hale.
He loves his home's children.
Also alcohol. Plato's dead.
Butchers are told by their knuckles,
As poets are told by love.

On top, all storeys up, if you walk out
On the roof as if doing something,
There are the ships,
The lambent air burdened with life tunes,
Little screaming and quiet symphonies,
Even in New York. O tall beautiful,
No, not sails any more, nor Queequegs:
Yet not too sullen steel plows,
And carriage like health. The
Colour of intestines fascinates.

I saw lungs like mackerel sunsets in Haiphong;
Smooth bladders the
Shade of evening's amber rain;
Hearts as of New Mexican earth,
When wet; all very carnelian.

Why love so long the even, but almost
Deathy darkness, that wells
Into dawn over buildings:
Opaque quietude, such tonal,
One mode. Why love so strong.
Perhaps because gentleness
Looks real (like death).
And the sun, when he comes glaring,
Is pain unending. Wrap around me,
Shroud of the dawn almost:
The sun with his eye will put out mine.
Sweet universal sky, seen
Through the sesame-slit of a dirty lavatory,
Where I wash my hands of hates.

I pretend I am the young Goya,
Enjoying fallow and burnished,
There, polyglot faces. His the bigger
German's, with hands oily to match,
Of matchless golden aura, dark
Enough, as in Rembrandt, too
Solid to be eclectic, no Goya;
But smoothest tempered skin all
Health, an animal pleasure,
Let us rejoice. Undangerous he,
Regular, in simplicity, without
Pride but humble in muscles
And can say "aw right" almost American.

John, Czecho-Slovakian competent,
Bites his hand in a steel door.

Incoming truck's the gorge, bitter
Teeth, and no fault. Pitiful
O my John, like a different man
With mind bemused and maimed,
John like a boy almost whimpers,
Waits upon sympathy. Puffed
Hands under warm water tap.
Huge arms capable of
Two hundred pounds hold the hurt
Hand as it were a flower;
Or a dead something.

There is some mournful music,
Somewhere, I give myself into
The slow god. Like a man
Grasping at peace, maelstromed
In this fourmillante cite.
Until sombrely, lovingly I close
In the doleful scales my being.
It is a whole world of direct power,
Now, intangible, being
So in solitude, seeming powerless.
But while in the thick pleasure
Not any says: experience
Lives as at a sea's depth,
In its darkness, surrounded
By itself, by itself filled,
Tonal tropism. I am
My own tonal tropism. I am.
The something done by dense
Minor, no lyric, oneness,
One sound, and essence of being,
Being without the object, yet
So surely oneself in spite of it.
Accordance of sympathy,
Equilibrium of the tempo composed
Of disparate things. All sorrow,

Let it be my shroud, in folds
Of music. Known in the heart's
Well, like standing in mud.

Embowelled again. Put the insides out.
This is a vast peristalsis:
Robbers dine on expectations,
In caves of hesitancies.
Sparse gigantic flecks of what might be snow;
Walk on murder trials to work. It is so cold;
Try over the buildings to the colder moon,
That same, for warmths, fires, flames of hell.
Not there, this dated night, can keep love
Out of mind, Sicilian singing.

In the lyric buoyance of this dull café,
She came into the café, walked to the back,
Sat with her back to the front
Of the room. The ugliest woman I'd
Ever laid eyes on,
Life to the viscera. Revulsion and vision spring.
Skin like malice, that makes her eyes unbearable.
Ripeness is gall. She spoiled my meal,
And a rat ran over my feet.

I thought they were all standing
Around like dead men,
So much physical life they had,
Who laboured among red substances.
They were dead men, so I mused
Among noises, silence the heat and
Cyclopean eye of vibrations,
Activity the opposite of whatever it is.
They were dead men, with big hands
Cooler-puffed, no life in them,
Continually I mused upon,
And amused me with this

Runlet of consciousness,
Confounded with the actual?
No life in them, but they were of life,
See still I fret about the mind.
But one might almost say their bodies thought,
In their honest and cool cells.

I have flung myself down into this pit.
Now they are all dead; statuesque
Stand these actors, these buildings
Building no more. Death I saw,
And wormed through it. And make fragment
Of the end of a time, when seethed
So thick the life, it knew not,
In savage complexity, modernity,
The harsh omnipotence of evil.

AESTHETICS AFTER WAR

(*To A. Nykyforcza,*
Student of Sighting.

The floating reticle became your eye,
You saw flashing battle,

You returned in the death lists.)

I PROPOSITIONS

Is the rose the same after it is seen?
Is it brighter if the seer has a blighted gall bladder?

If a poet is colour blind, either by nature,
Or say by choice,
So that his deep wish to see purple
Gives him constitutionally a purple world,
As the romanticist finds excess where others

Do not find it,
As the classical scholar finds the world more classical
Than any striking steel worker knows it,
As the aesthetician finds the world
An aesthete's paradigm, to whom then
The pleasure principle is the end of all,
Do the poet, the romanticist, the classicist, the aesthetician
By their profound aberration
Discover the true reality of nature?

What is the relation of aesthetics to philosophy?
Should there be any?
Is its branch an authentic olive tree?
If you contemplate the rose, do you have to think about it?
If you achieve a beatific state
In the contemplation of the rose
Are you loving wisdom?
Is it possible to achieve abstract purity,
The ultimate knowledge of the object rose,
Without a mystical infiltration?
Should an aesthetician wish to think?
Should a thinking aesthetician want to know God?
Will God appear in the ultimate stillness of the rose?

Keats confused, confounded two centuries
By ambivalent, ambiguous
Mating of truth with beauty.
Or are these absolutes safe in unattainability?
So that the searcher, as centuries ago,
May struggle, physically, logically, semantically,
Or by purposive derangement of the senses
To find them, being relatively certain
Their abstraction will inhere and remain
Long after his bones have turned to very earth?

What has the aesthetics to do with society?
Was the Italian airman crazy

When he saw aesthetic purity
In bombs flowering like roses a mile below?
He could not see nor feel the pain of man.
Our own men testify to awe,
If not to aesthetic charm,
On seeing man's total malice over Hiroshima,
That gigantic, surrealistic, picture-mushroom
And objectification of megalomania.
A world of men who butcher men
In the arsenical best interests of several states,
The modern warring maniacal man,
Is this world of men inimical
To the postulates of the study aesthetics?

II INSTRUMENTS

There are many intricate pieces of workmanship,
Precise instruments like the Mark 18 Sight,
With a floating reticle and a fixed reticle,
The fixed being a circle of light with a cross at the centre,
The floating being eight brilliant diamond points of light
In a broken circle which enlarges and contracts
Framing the enemy wingspan, increasing
As the enemy plane comes nearer, grows larger,
Decreasing as it flies away, grows smaller,
The whole floating reticle a dream of beauty,
But accurate to a split second of gunfire,
Its gyroscopic precision solving all problems
Of boresight, the pursuit curve,
Of wind drift, range, of bullet pattern
So that as semi-automaton all the young gunner
Has to do is to frame the enemy plane
In this brilliant circle of light and blaze away.
This is one of a bewildering array of imaginations.
Radar, as another expression of ingenious invention,
In its excessive, but already dated modernity,
Only gives man what bats have used for centuries,

Whose vibrations, beyond the reach of the human ear,
Strike obstacles which echo back to warn the bat
Who instantly evades each thing that would harm,
Although he seems to us to employ erratic flight.

Warfare spurs man to electrify himself with technics
But never can the human be contraverted
And as the Mark 18 Sight is only the fastest
Eye in the fastest brain, the perfectly anticipatory one,
And as radar is only an equal intelligence
To the ancient, instinctive knowledge of the bat,
So mankind in his abrasive rigors
Constructing the mazes of his complex aircraft
Often unwittingly makes them look like huge
Beetles or other insects, and I have seen
Hundreds of Corsairs parked in the evening glow
Their wings folded back ethereal as butterflies.
If a floating reticle in an electrical sight,
If a radar screen with its surrealistic eeriness,
If an airplane poised on the ground like a butterfly
Are beautiful, is their beauty incidental?
Is it man's limitation that his mechanical creations
Perforce cannot escape from his manhood?
And that try as he will, his works are human
And never stray far from the functions of the natural?
The mystery is whether the object
Mystifies man,
Or whether the mysteriousness within man
Transubstantiates the object;
Whether the world is finally mysterious,
Or if the Deity has put a mystery in man.

III THE PULL OF MEMORY

Each argument begets its counterpart,
Only in opposites the truth is human,
Intelligible, the shoemaker Boehme said.

I recall a steamer on the Pearl River
Slipping out from teeming Canton,
Hong Kong outward bound through swarming sampans,
The glow of the East, the intense hot day,
The swan sweep of the boat on swan-swept water,
The lull of the hours in the yellow afternoon,
I remember walking the deck
Watching the ritual of the opium eaters
Through glassless windows in the inner sanctum,
Sensing their subtle gestures and serene manners
Through the prolonged trance of the opium haze;
Then looking out, on the banks of the Pearl River
Ancient of days, and of centuries,
There stood a tall pagoda old as the memories of China.
So Buddha seemed in the soft air to dwell,
Incomparably indwelling, selfless and whole,
Without action, away from world's suffering.
And I was stolen in a trance
Of the pagoda like a jewel in ancient, shimmering air,
And of the mild-eyed Chinese recumbent after smoking,
Mysterious inducements of the suffusing scene.

In the East contemplation is a self-annihilation,
In the West it never escapes intrusive action.

IV REALITY

The tail, the waist, the nose turret or the ball gunner,
Using the sight with floating reticle
Has only, if his work is properly done,
Has only to press the trigger. The enemy explodes in the air.
It is all so fast sometimes
Neither pilot nor gunner can see the result,
Until, far up and away
Banking over, high above the blue ocean
They glimpse far below pieces of plane
Drift idly, suspended in the air.

But reality is there.
Death is the reality in this case,
Love is the reality of St. Theresa,
Identification is the reality of Boehme,
For Blake innocence and experience
Were indistinguishable in mystical affinity,
Our enemy pilot was dead by a death-dealing pounce
Of superior machinery and superior manoeuvre and aim—
But what Chance was there!—
For in battle, as if man were made of adrenalin
There is no time for fear or fault, for faith or fame
But pilots say it is all like a football game.
Back on the carrier their hearts may pound,
After the event, when significance comes,
But up in the air intense and free
Controlled and able,
Perfectly secure,
What is the end of a man
You never saw before,
You never see?

It is the end of this man whose life yours never touched,
Of whose existence you never knew,
Young man, young man,
Whose floating corpse you will never view,
Whose friends you also slew,
It is the end of this man,
Or let us say it is the end of Man
Christ shed his blood for,
He shed His blood for you.

He knew you, savage trickster,
Your accomplished guile,
The total ignorance of your intelligent blasphemy,
The evil that is ineradicable
He died to show.

He would redeem the enemy airman's blood-muffled scream,
He would redeem the pride of your indifferent victory.

Is there any doubt that Christ was the most aesthetic man?
As aetheticism is a part of philosophy,
Philosophy a part of life,
Life action, for even the Nirvana-seeker still breathes,
And Stylites pulls up food in a basket,
So Christ contemplated the ultimate origin,
But originated the ultimate rules of action.
All things are interlocked, interlaced,
Interinvolved, interdenominated.
The pilot who pinched himself in his bomber,
Because only a year ago he was a boy in school,
Hardly realizing the magnitude of his change,
Was only one of a squadron,
A flying integer in a welter of heterogeneity.
Christ belonged to the Jewish race
But Chinese and Japanese speak to Him now.

The poet is a man of sense
Who handles the brightness of the air,
The viewless tittles he dandles,
Timelessness is his everywhere.

His blood is in the rose he contemplates
The blood of the rose reddens in his mind,
The poet is master of presences,
He is the insight of the blind.

Poetry is so mad and so kind
It is so majestic an inventive surprise,
Is it any wonder that in it
The spirit of man arise?

ON SHOOTING PARTICLES BEYOND
THE WORLD

"White Sands, N.M. Dec. 18 (UP). 'We first throw a little something into the skies,' Zwicky said. 'Then a little more, then a shipload of instruments—then ourselves'."

On this day man's disgust is known
Incipient before but now full blown
With minor wars of major consequence,
Duly building empirical delusions.

Now this little creature in a rage
Like new-born infant screaming compleat angler
Objects to the whole globe itself
And with a vicious lunge he throws

Metal particles beyond the orbit of mankind.
Beethoven shaking his fist at death,
A giant dignity in human terms,
Is nothing to this imbecile metal fury.

The world is too much for him. The green
Of earth is not enough, love's deities,
Peaceful intercourse, happiness of nations,
The wild animal dazzled on the desert.

If the maniac would only realize
The comforts of his padded cell
He would have penetrated the
Impenetrability of the spiritual.

It is not intelligent to go too far.
How he frets that he can't go too!
But his particles would maim a star,
His free-floating bombards rock the moon.

Good Boy! We pat the baby to eructate,
We pat him then for eructation.
Good Boy Man! Your innards are put out,
From now all space will be your vomitorium.

The atom bomb accepted this world,
Its hatred of man blew death in his face.
But not content, he'll send slugs beyond,
His particles of intellect will spit on the sun.

Not God he'll catch, in the mystery of space.
He flaunts his own out-cast state
As he throws his imperfections outward bound,
And his shout that gives a hissing sound.

A LEGEND OF VIABLE WOMEN

I

Maia was one, all gold, fire, and sapphire,
Bedazzling of intelligence that rinsed the senses,
She was of Roman vocables the disburser,
Six courtiers in Paris sat to her hats.

There was Anna, the cool Western evidencer
Who far afield sought surrender in Sicily,
Wept under the rose window of Palma de Mallorca,
For she thought fate had played a child in her hand.

There was Betty the vigorous; her Packard of Philadelphia
Spurred she; she was at home in Tanganyika,
Who delighted to kill the wild elephant,
Went Eastward on, to the black tigers of Indochine.

There was Margaret of Germany in America, and Jerusalem,
Of mild big eyes, who loved the blood of Englishmen,
Safely to voyage the Eros battlements of Europe,
Protectress to be of young and home, massive the mother.

There was Helen the blond Iowan, actress raddled,
Who dared learning a little, of coyness the teacher,
Laughing subtleties, manipulator of men, a Waldorf
Of elegant fluff, endangering to the serious.

There was Jeannette the cool and long, bright of tooth,
Lady of gay friendship, and of authentic song,
Beyond and indifferent to the male seduction
Who to art pledged all her nature's want and call.

There was the sultry Emma of West Virginia,
Calf-eyed, velvet of flesh, mature in youngness,
Gentle the eager learner of nature's dimensions,
Always to her controlling womanhood in thrall.

There was Sue, the quick, the artful, the dashing,
Who broke all the laws; a Villager in her own apartment,
She was baffled by the brains of Plato and Aristotle,
Whose mind contained most modern conceptions.

There was Maxine, a woman of fire and malice
Who knew of revenge and subterfuge the skills,
A dominator, a thin beauty, a woman of arts and letters;
She of many psychological infidelities.

There was savage Catherine, who leaped into the underground,
Her female anger thrown at abstract injustice.
And she could match her wits with international man,
A glory, a wreaker, alas, who now posthumous is.

There was Madge the sinister, who raged through husbands
     three.
She was somdel Groddeckian, a spendthrift of morality;
Existentialist that with men was dexterous
And would be in ten years after thirty, thirty-three.

There was a nun of modesty, who with service was heavy
And big with sweet acts all her sweet life long;
Enough wisdom she had for twenty ordinary women
Who percepted love as a breath, and as a song.

II

Where is Kimiko, the alabaster girl of Tokyo,
Living in bamboo among rustling scents and innuendoes,
To whom from Hatteras, the Horn, or Terra del Fuego
Returned as to a starry placement the sea voyager?

Where has time cyclic eventuated Vera
The proud noblewoman of Vienna? Among opera lights
She lived in a gaiety of possessive disasters,
Abandoned to the retaliatory shores of music.

Where is the naked brown girl of the nipa hut,
Under fronds, to Mount Mayon's perfect symmetry,
From the wash of the sea, looking from Legaspi?
Where in nature is this form, so brown, so fair, so free?

Where, who, sold into slavery in white Shanghai,
Walked and breathed in grace on Bubbling Well Road,
Subject to ancient sinuosities and patience,
Whose power was to represent unquestioning obedience?

Where is Hortense, the hermetically sealed?
Where is Hermione, haunted by heavens, who hesitated?
Where is Lucy, of bees and liberty the lover?
Where is Eustacia, of marionettes and Austrian dolls?

III

There were prideful women; women of blood and lust;
Patient women who rouged with scholarship's dust;
There were women who touched the soul of the piano;
Women as cat to mouse with their psychoanalyst.

There were women who did not understand themselves
Locking and unlocking misery's largess yearly;
Fabulous women who could not manumit the world
And babbled in syllables of the past and of money.

There were women committed to sins of treachery
The aborters of privilege and of nature's necessity;
There were the sinners in acedia of frigidity
Who negated even the grossness and grandeur of fear.

There were women without tenderness or pity
There were those more male than feminine men
Who rode the horses of their strident fury,
To whom subtle time made a passing bow.

There were independent women of society
Whose proud wisdom was their father's will.
There were mysterious women, Egyptian as a scarab
To whom scent and sound were a mysterious recall.

IV

Women are like the sea, and wash upon the world
In unalterable tides under the yellowing moon
Whose essential spirit is like nature's own,
To man the shadowy waters, the great room.

They come and go in tides of passion, and show
The melancholy at the heart of fullness,
Time crumples them, these vessels of the generations
Are crushed on the rocks as the green sea urchins.

They are the flesh in its rich, watery symbol,
A summer in July under the tenderest moon,
An island in the sea invincible to touch,
A refuge in man against refulgent ideation.

133

Women have gone where roll the sea bells
In the long, slow, the wide and the clear waters;
Their flesh which is our love and our loss
Has become the waste waters of the ocean swell.

They are the mothers of man's intelligence
To whom he is held by umbilical time,
And far though he roam, to treat with imagination,
He is brought home to her, as she brings a child.

THE VERBALIST OF SUMMER

I

The verbalist, with colours at his hand,
In the events and size of volant summer,
Thought at the sea's edge
How to wash the sovereign waters;

They were in a grandeur of the actual
And they leaped upon his eyes in tunes
That broke from island hills in blues
And flashed across the waves in mauves.

Is this the sea that balks my verbalism,
The mediator said, by flying hyalines,
Is this sea actual? Is this the real sea?
For he was the register of reality.

Or is it a chasm where old bones are rolled;
Forced peace with roaring rollers made
In the mad tangles of sea bells, fog, fate,
That specific for the forecast of our doom?

Or is it, while his nimble fingers flexed
The dawns, the sunsets of old centuries,

Awaiting the charms of elegance, of synthesis
Which ones to use, which tones to blend,

Is it the subtle messenger of nature
Hidden in the complexity of Psyche
That here appears, and are these bells, these shades
The temper of our mysterious complicity?

Was the water factual? Was it actual?
Did the eyes deceive, and did the senses drown
His too attentive blood in sudden frenzies
That made a music rare and rich in air?

He had the colour harmonies at hand
In the calm vegetation of his eyes;
In the aural cavities of carved sea rock
The rhythmic knowledge of neap certainties.

The verbalist, in all this wealth and scale,
Kept looking at the laughing, dappling water,
Hypnotic to the last, until his vision ceased,
And clearly then he saw that he was natural

To the menacing and the loving sea,
His intellect a super-imposition;
The verbalist sat in dells of verbalism,
As in a flower field, with music in the air,

And he made the sea level with his eyes,
No longer in the power of the imponderables.
All that mystery of the washing waters
Dissolved within his mortal reality.

II

The sea is mine, I am the sea,
For I am human if I am anything,

And I am the master of what I see,
Said to himself the cogent verbalist.

I am what I dream, the waters that I make
Are dreams of summer-scented splendours;
They are the dawns that stir the cormorants
Across the brightening ledges, and the gulls'

Elaborate conclamations. They are the loons'
Curious litanies, and the high osprey's cry.
I dream the waters, and I make the sea
Responsible; for I am what I take and make.

Subjective sea, sea of the deep sea-wish,
Waters of the blood that wash the world,
I claim the element of size and tone
My own, I make the sea, I am the sea;

Stylization of objects, fixation of dreams,
Compendium of imponderables,
Visionary screen on which is played
The magic games of the soul's reality.

So said the viewing verbalist
By the side of the ocean segment,
Mindful and instructed that he
Was, actually, foreign to this element.

And knowing that, where eyes were wide
To so many occult divergencies
His tones and colours were his own
The sundial sea was the plastic timepiece

As it had been when he began his reverie
And would be ten thousand years from now,
A living nature beyond the realm of art,
Try as poetry does to have it poetry.

III

I must begin again, the verbalist said.
The sea is always getting out of hand;
It is an addict of the summer's chances.
Those air-dances on the water, there, he said.

I must arrange the props, theorize
The distances and densities, defend
The subtlest of shifting elucidations.
The sea is a subject of some malfeasance.

He began to brim with violent intensities.
He saw a savage power, the ships broken up;
He had not thought so changeable a source
Could violate so many presumed images.

Accept the historians too; and of the weather
The weather-makers. And of sea-power
Its expositors and rampant individualists;
And place just so the salmon canneries.

The dullness of the ritual lighthouse keepers;
The thickening of the salt by centuries.
Typhoons, unseen, in the pacific sea;
Scott tying up to the Great Ice Barrier.

He began to think it was too much,
The subject proliferous and cantankerous,
No medicine to the subsuming spirit
Of order, gall to the onlooker, a tempest.

To be didactic about the ocean
Is to be a child, the verbalist said.
What does the child see in the ocean?
He sees the bright pebbles by the shore.

CONCORD CATS

The soft cat and the scratchy cat
Have milk in cold blue plates.
Then, in evenings, star-cool evenings
Equal to their reticence,
Emblems of independence,

These China cats, of black and white,
Will go on planetary pads
Uphill, where crouch
On eighteenth-, seventeenth-century
Houses, the graves of Concord.

By pious inscriptions
That antedate the Revolution
They see, through eyes cold and chaste,
The scratchy cat, the soft cat,
With humour old and Oriental,

That nature is meant for poise.
Battles, bloodshed, death,
Are men mirroring time,—
The stars blue, the night paling—
Are data. Imperviousness. Integrity.

ON THE FRAGILITY OF MIND

Mind is a most delicate evidence.
Not a soul has seen it yet.
And yet I think it is dense,
Although of great expense.

I suspect it of all trickery,
The master of the greatest paradoxes.
It is the historian of the world,
Crafty and foxy.

Old entablatures in Venice remind me
Of the mind of Tintoretto or Veronese.
These came to a watery nothingness
But for the golden paint I see.

I think there is no mind at all,
Perhaps, but only desires and faiths,
And the great capability of art
Which shows us forms, divine.

GREAT PRAISES

Great praises of the summer come
With the flushed hot air
Burdening the branches.

Great praises are in the air!
For such a heat as this
We have sweated out our lives toward death.

I used to hate the summer ardour
In all my intellectual pride,
But now I love the very order

That brushed me fast aside,
And rides upon the air of the world
With insolent, supernal splendour.

THE DRY ROT

The fine powder of the dry rot,
A new texture in the heart of the wood,
Crooked my finger as I scooped it out,
The rare old stuff of mankind's dream.

What to do with it? Pure contemplation?
Savage remorse? Illimitable irony?

A cosmetic for the face of Cleopatra?
Time in the blood is this pale substance too.

I mixed it with my sweat, and painted on
My legs and biceps bands of gold.
Sallying forth in the guise of Anthony
I sought the dusky land of sandy Egypt.

With a savage queen I lost remorse;
I threw my manhood down along a gold divan.
With a gesture of defiance and of loss
I met the meaning of the dry rot in that land.

Dig me up, then, in some later century,
Threading the pale sand through your thin fingers.
As you unclothe my bones in scholarship's delight,
Think of dialetic, imagination, the Rose of Venus.

THE SKIER AND THE MOUNTAIN

The gods are too airy: feathery as the snow
When its consistency is just the imagination's,
I recognize, but also in an airy, gauzy way
That it will capture me, I will never capture it.
The imagination is too elusive, too like me.
The gods are the airiness of my spirit.
I have dreamed upon them tiptop dreams,
Yet they elude me, like the next step on the ski.
I pole along, push upward, I see the summit,
Yet the snow on which I glide is treachery.
The gods are too airy. It is their elusive nature
I in my intellectual pride have wished to know.
I have thought I knew what I was doing,
Gliding over the cold, resisting element,
Toward some summit all my strength could take.
The gods are the fascination of the place, they escape
The genius of the place they make. They evade

The blood of our question. Imagination is a soaring,
It never allows the firm, inevitable step.
The gods tantalize me, and the gods' imaginations.
I am thus the captured actor, the taken one,
The used, I am used up by the will of the gods,
I am their imagination, lost to self and to will.
In this impossibility is my humility.

I saw an old country god of the mountain,
Far up, leaning out of the summit mist,
Born beyond time, and wise beyond our wisdom.
He was beside an old, gnarled trunk of a tree
Blasted by the winds. Stones outcropped the snow,
There where the summit was bare, or would be bare.
I thought him a dream-like creature, a god beyond evil,
And thought to speak of the portent of my time,
To broach some ultimate question. No bird
Flew in this flying mist. As I raised my voice
To shape the matters of the intellect
And integrate the spirit, the old, wise god,
Natural to the place, positive and free,
Vanished as he had been supernatural dream.
I was astonished by his absence, deprived
Of the astonishment of his presence, standing
In a reverie of the deepest mist, cloud and snow,
Solitary on the mountain slope: the vision gone,
Even as the vision came. This was then the gods' meaning,
That they leave us in our true humanity,
Elusive, shadowy gods of our detachment,
Who lead us to the summits, and keep their secrets.

THE HUMAN BEING IS A
LONELY CREATURE

It is borne in upon me that pain
Is essential. The bones refuse to act.
Recalcitrancy is life's fine flower.
The human being is a lonely creature.

Fear is of the essence. You do not fear?
I say you lie. Fear is the truth of time.
If it is not now, it will come hereafter.
Death is waiting for the human creature.

Praise to harmony and love.
They are best, all else is false.
Yet even in love and harmony
The human being is a lonely creature.

The old sloughed off, the new new-born,
What fate and what high hazards join
As life tries out the soul's enterprise.
Time is waiting for the human creature.

Life is daring all our human stature.
Death looks, and waits for each bright eye.
Love and harmony are our best nurture.
The human being is a lonely creature.

THE BOOK OF NATURE

As I was reading the book of nature
In the fall of the year
And picking the full blueberries
Each as round as a tear;

As I was being in my boyhood
Scanning the book of the rocks,
Intercepting the wrath to come
Where the hay was in the shocks;

As I was eye-drinking the waters
As they came up Seal Cove
With the eyes of my dazzled daughter,
An absolutist of a sudden grove;

As I was on that sea again
With islands stretching off the sail,
The real sea of mysterious time,
Islands of summer storm and hail;

As I was living with the love of death,
A concentrated wonder of the birches,
Passionate in the shudder of the air
And running on the splendour of the waters;

As I was a person in the sea birds,
And I was a spirit of the ferns,
And I was a dream of the monadnocks,
An intelligence of the flocks and herds;

As I was a memory of memory,
Keeper of the holy seals,
The unified semblance of disparates
And wielder of the real;

As I was happy as the ospreys,
As I was full of broom and bright afflatus,
As I was a vehicle of silence
Being the sound of a sudden hiatus;

As I was the purified exemplar
And sufferer of the whole adventure,

And as I was desire in despair,
A bird's eye in doom's nature;

As I stood in the whole, immaculate air,
Holding all things together,
I was blessed in the knowledge of nature.
God is man's weather.

Then I saw God on my fingertip
And I was glad for all who ever lived,
Serene and exalted in mood,
Whatever the mind contrived.

Then God provided an answer
Out of the overwhelming skies and years
And wrath and judgment then and there
Shook out the human tears.

COUSIN FLORENCE

There it is, a block of leaping marble
Given to me by an ancestor.
The hands that passed it held down ninety years.
She got it in the love-time of Swinburne.

This woman with her stalwart mien,
More like a Roman than a Greek,
Fumbled among old bags of rubble
For something indomitable that she could seek.

She saw the light of ancient days around her,
Calling in the hip-cracked hospital.
She chose at last. Then the clear light
Of reason stood up strong and tall.

With a pure, commanding grace
She handed me a piece of the Parthenon,

Saying, this I broke with my own hands,
And gave me the imagination of the Greeks.

I thought the spirit of this woman
The tallest that I had ever seen,
Stronger than the marble that I have,
Who was herself imagination's dream

By the moment of such sacrament,
A pure force transmitting love,
Endurance, steadfastness, her calm,
Her Roman heart, to mine, of dream.

I would rather keep her noble acts,
The blood of her powerful character, a mind
As good as any of her time, than search
My upward years for such a stone that leaps.

SESTINA

I die, no matter what I do I die.
Is this the sum of what man has to do?
There is no use to fly to be at ease.
Man flies, but knows not what he does.
It is in war you want to be in peace.
In Heaven, in Heaven I want to be in Hell.

The mortal span to find out Heaven and Hell!
No matter what I have to do I die,
The gods comply to cancel you to peace.
Before this then what is it man should do?
And after, does it matter what he does?
Will Christ-like Christ then put him at his ease?

Will will will him his own, a fabled ease?
Will, some say, is the whole road to Hell.
But man is bound to Hell whatever he does.

No matter what he does he has to die.
It is the dying that you have to do
Defies the hyaline lustre of the peace.

Despair has not the end in view of peace
Nor has desire the purposes of ease,
But action, while you live, is what's to do.
Thought is three crossed roads that lead to Hell,
Your thought is fatal and will make you die,
For thinking kills as much as action does.

It is not what he thinks, nor what he does
Nor what cold mystery of the Prince of Peace
Avails—no matter what I do I die,
May nothing, nothing put me at my ease
Except the reality of Heaven and Hell.
No one told me what I ought to do.

The scriptures told you what you ought to do.
They are unreasonable truth, and what man does
Believe when most he believes in Heaven and Hell.
That passes understanding, that is peace.
But sky-fallen man will not be put at ease.
I die, no matter what I do I die.

No matter what I do I have no peace.
No matter what man does he has no ease.
Heaven and Hell are changeless when I die.

'MY GOLDEN AND MY FIERCE ASSAYS'

My golden and my fierce assays,
My bold and sudden thunderbolts,
My costly lights, have led me all astray
And cut the ground from hope.

My will was avid, and my force
Commingling love and aspiration;
And my animal nature held
To auras of and beams of creation.

Wisdom comes in the short hours of night.
He came with the armed song of man
And I was destroyed in my light
In the coldest, daftest night.

For he said, the will is evil,
You live within a blind delight.
Violence is a fine delight,
Faith sang above the fight!

UR BURIAL

Reach me a blue pencil of the moon,
The double-reined rings from tombs of Ur,
The lyre, the javelins from Sumer,
'The Ram caught in a thicket.'

A gold dagger, a golden toilet case,
The gold helmet of Meskalam-dug;
Rein-ring and mascot from
Queen Shub-ad's chariot.

I will drink a narcotic rich and dark,
I will lie down by my master in his sarcophagus,
All our company will join in sleep
To serve the sun in a life beyond sleep.

SEEING IS DECEIVING

Having fed impalpably on the ineluctable
In yearlong passion of the unfathomed,
To realign the mystery of the ineffable,

Haltingly, haltingly, in lofty clashes,
Longsight glare, in total psychic refusal,
He would not allow his eyes to see the rose.

The rose that is with blood transfused,
The rose absolute, rose of all the world,
Flower of the flesh, flesh of the very flower,

Intruding organ of most rage-potential sense,
Rich rugged rose, the years in their dark make,
Sagest blossoms that can break and bless,

He would not in a high perfection sit,
Staring the day away in anarchy
That saw a heaven in imperfection's makeshifts,

And told the world in the etcher's fine escape,
The gardens clamant in the blare of June,
Birds precise, clouds fixed, grasses interlaced

With grasses as they are, and nature had,
But crying against perfection of the sight
He broke perfection with the inner eye,

Sombre, strange, amorphous, vast, replete,
And all his organs in the dark of time
Created the secret of an ultimatum.

ANALOGUE OF UNITY IN MULTEITY

A man of massive meditation
Is like a man looking at death,
Looking at death as at a bull's-eye.
He watches before he crosses the tracks.

Every day a man is in a box,
Hourly he watches the trains go by,

Opening and closing the wooden gates,
As one who is interested in the world.

The man who is massive in thought,
As it were of mountainous fortitude,
Whom decades have seasoned in male beauty,
Whose clarity is an age of harmony,

A man of intellectual power
Will not be killed by a ribboned artifice.
He is too full of deaths to be undone,
Death is his hourly communion.

Who will say what the gate-keeper thinks?
A man necessary to the metropolis,
Comfort he knows, he keeps a comfort station,
As decades pass on shining steel.

The meditative man, a power of eye,
Big shouldered, with the torso of a Jove,
Is master of a world of action,
An actor in a world of masks.

In complex thought he walks along
The most fearless man to be seen,
For with animal nature he is one,
Who looks ever death in the bull's-eye.

Far in the sky another eye
Beholds these creatures in their ways,
Indifferent to their differences,
A point of agate reference.

SEA-HAWK

The six-foot nest of the sea-hawk,
Almost inaccessible,
Surveys from the headland the lonely, the violent waters.

I have driven him off,
Somewhat foolhardily,
And look into the fierce eye of the offspring.

It is an eye of fire,
An eye of icy crystal,
A threat of ancient purity,

Power of an immense reserve,
An agate-well of purpose,
Life before man, and maybe after.

How many centuries of sight
In this piercing, inhuman perfection
Stretch the gaze off the rocky promontory,

To make the mind exult
At the eye of a sea-hawk,
A blaze of grandeur, permanence of the impersonal.

SAINTE ANNE DE BEAUPRÉ

The sun saw on that widening shore
Three hundred mothers with their daughters.
All dressed in white they followed slowly
Their mothers to the great stone doors.

O Bonne Sainte Anne
O Bonne Sainte Anne
The priest intoned upon the electric air.

The wind was bright from hundred years
And bright from off that distant shore
As slowly walked the maidens with
Their mothers to the cold church door.

A spectacle of heavenly imagery
And sun and wind upon the place,
The slow procession seemed a dream of time
While loudly through the air the cry implored

O Bonne Sainte Anne
O Bonne Sainte Anne,
Protectress of these children in their time.

Bronze on the hill, beyond the heavy Church
Stood dark the Stations of the Cross
In groves deep hidden from the sight
And from the brightness of such angelance.

O Bonne Sainte Anne,
O Bonne Sainte Anne,
Loudspoken tone upon white-flowing air.

Three hundred maidens beside their mothers
Slowly mount the tributary steps,
Entering to receive the blessing
Thought beyond all human ill.

O Bonne Sainte Anne!
O Bonne Sainte Anne!
An ancient spell lifts high in air!

And slowly came at last with blessings
And slowly down the prospect walked
And formed a slow and long procession
Of sun and wind and timeless innocence.

O Bonne Sainte Anne,
O Bonne Sainte Anne,

Protect the young in their extremity,
The wish of men who know all evil.

Such ecstasy had filled the hearts of many
And made so glad the light of tender eyes
It is a hurt that dream is not eternity,
And Bonne Sainte Anne not hunted down by time.

MEDITERRANEAN SONG

I like to see, when I am low,
The form I had when I was strong.

I charged the battlements of Carcassonne,
I climbed the white slopes of the tempting Etna

Startling the nymphs from the blue grottoes, the cool.
Transmitting new sanctions oblique and jocund

I threw my weight about the Mediterranean
In the true theatre of the antique world.

Almost a satyr in the woods, I was;
Almost Socrates in the market place.

TO EVAN

I wanted to give him some gift,
The breath of my breath, the look of my eyes,
I wanted to give him some gift,
Lying there so piteously.

I wanted to give him some gift,
Small child dying slowly,
With brave blue intelligent eyes,
His form withered piteously.

Only in the intelligence of those eyes
Where life had retreated for a piercing look
Was the enormous mystery justified,
As he inhaled the betraying oxygen.

I wanted to give him some gift,
A look from my look not to frighten him,
A breath from my haleness, my even vigour,
The same breath as his lonely breath.

Tenacious life in this little form
That will soon vanish from it entirely,
Unforgettable features of this little boy,
Do you mock my passion in your long passing?

I wanted to give him some gift,
Breath of my breath, the look of my eyes,
This is all upon earth, under heaven,
I can give him, a child dying, and I unwise.

Though I would menace the tall skies
And cry out as man has from the beginning
At the unequal fate held over us from our birth
I could not for a moment suspend this child's dying.

O though I would look into his intelligent eyes
With the world's weight of experience and despair
I could not mate the black look before death,
Nor seize the secret from the secrecy.

I wanted to give him some gift,
Breath of my breath, the look of my eyes.
Farewell, fair spirit. Fare forward, voyager.
I pass away silently and see him no more.

153

THE DAY-BED

I

It is green, it is made of willow.
I am baffled: I cannot think about it.
An obsession of twenty-seven years.
I am brutalized to look upon it.

The very form of love. Of time
The essence, which is memory.
The flash of light, and a long sleep.
This is the bed of day, and night.

No, but soft, but untold love
Arises. The very heart of love!
So long ago that suffering form
Slowly grew to death through pain,

Here on this very furniture.
It seems impossible. Time lies.
I do not see her lying there,
Great eyes, great gray-black hair.

I do not see that agonizing stare
That's deep through all my nights and days,
Substratum of the flying years;
The great pain without a cure.

II

Reality is a passing thing.
The Day-Bed lives, remains, reminds
Of the eternity of change
To this same, writing finger.

The emblem remains, bounteous gift,
The strange, pure gift of memory,

A blooded drench, a flushed presentiment;
And throngs and throngs of images.

Day-Bed of Life-in-Death,
That while my eyes shall change and see,
I look upon this furniture,
The not estranging imagery.

And summon up the love, and see
The very form and flesh of love
As it is with all mankind,
The loves long lost, the loves most near.

Who cursed the blood within the veins
Appareling day with source of night
Shall dream upon a lovely dream
Though the deep heart choke, and fight.

III

It is green, it is made of willow.
Lithe winds of Spring wave over it.
It is a new time and a new day,
New flesh here springs in harmony,

Laughs and tumbles and is gay.
Is gay! Is lithe as wings of Spring
And bends to nature as a willow
Triumphing in its green, cool stay.

Two lovers here electing unity
Flaunt eclectic idols in the day,
Consuming the great world of sense,
And laughing in its careless sway.

They sway. They laugh. And leaping
Loosen the mind from iron prisons,
Celebrating speeds of instancy
In vernal cells of intimacy.

Green and willowy marriage time!
Time of the beliefless flesh!
Time of the charges of the ruddy blood,
Joy that is swift and free, pure joy.

IV

Other years and other foils
Requite the ancient mysteries,
Persuading of some subtle balance
Between the losing and the winning battles,

Here on this very furniture,
Day-Bed of Life-in-Death!
A child plays in boisterous industry,
Truth off the old bones of mating.

Embroiled in fate he does not know,
Smiling mischievous and saintly,
Evidently impossible to quell,
The very future in his active eye,

The willowy Day-Bed of past time
That taught death in the substratum
Couches now the bliss of man,
A bright shape, a green new dream.

FORMATIVE MASTERSHIP

Never be happy until the golden hour
Creates its living death upon the instant
Just beyond perception: be happy then,
That you shall never understand that radiant
Mastery. It is gone as soon as known,
Known only as a breath of incalculable spirit,
Wordless peak except verbs prick at it;
Perhaps never known, but in this mating time.

156

Never be broken by the things of evil
That pass upon the years to true forgetfulness,
Giving themselves back to nature; man's evil
Forget, for in time forget you must,
Whether man wrought them from his crooked heart,
Or life imposed them in a cruel majesty
Impersonal and blind. Do not shake the fist
Or cry the brutal rage: time heals the time.

Baffled by instances of malice, keep
The calm of solitary imaginings,
That harmony inhere although the flesh be maimed,
Keep struggle pure with a white intent,
Revising possibility. Pare the naked nature
And in dark hours accept what fate is.
What toys we are to crippling chance
When victim, not the callers, of a savage dance.

Look upon the passing scene with tenderness.
All suffers change. The blight is in the air,
Within the lungs, within the light, within
The eye. Great nature is our master.
All our will and our flushed, enticed brains
Cannot unmake the world. Talk to the night
When the woods are deep, the stars alight.
Talk out the long instancy of mankind.

THE HAND AND THE SHADOW

The hand penetrated an abyss of shadow
When I came to the fullness of my being.
The shadow followed the hand in its search
Then leaped out of bounds, as if it were freeing

Itself from a compulsion and a tumulus;
And as if it wished to form new shapes,

157

And command a function of new elegance,
And as if it had the dignity of grapes;

This shadow that would escape the lordly hand,
And would break the bonds of its condition,
And be a fruit just at the point of bursting,
When meaning leaks from commission in emission;

This shadow now transfigured and as of flesh
That has in it the blood of memory,
And as of all blood that has in it action,
And rises in imagination's cheek as primary,

This shadow is now the grape at an exquisite point,
On a day of Autumn, the fullness of the year,
The hand has become something departed from,
And sits upon a symbol, as a tear

Breeds upon the eyelid of a natural action,
And bursts upon the fields of contemplation,
And, rich with death, and then with resurrection,
Sows a radiance round about the nation,

Then, as a glory pens the eye of man,
The shadow-semblance of a heavenly sun,
Comes back to humble energies and potence,
And the shadow and the hand are one.

WORDS

First a word was fuzzy, and was nothing.
It had all India in fee.
It had to do with illusion's very self
And nothing to do with me.

Then a word was mighty, and flew away,
An eagle on a rocky shelf;

It glowered over our America,
Depleting the inner self.

Finally a word was elegant and sheer,
Like the fabric of a stuff
Durable with the fate of things,
When I had lived enough.

Then I had a total myth
Sounding on an eternal shore.
It was the world-memory alone
When I was dead and gone.

ON A SQUIRREL CROSSING THE ROAD
IN AUTUMN, IN NEW ENGLAND

It is what he does not know,
Crossing the road under the elm trees,
About the mechanism of my car,
About the Commonwealth of Massachusetts,
About Mozart, India, Arcturus,

That wins my praise. I engage
At once in whirling squirrel-praise.

He obeys the orders of nature
Without knowing them.
It is what he does not know
That makes him beautiful.
Such a knot of little purposeful nature!

I who can see him as he cannot see himself
Repose in the ignorance that is his blessing.

It is what man does not know of God
Composes the visible poem of the world.

                  . . . Just missed him!

CENTENNIAL FOR WHITMAN

(Amimetobion, not Synapothanumenon)

I

What shall I say to Walt Whitman tonight?
Reading him here in the springtime of bursting green,
Foreign from him, held by the same air he breathed of the
    world,
Looking at night to the same stars, white and radiant,
Obsessed with a kindred obsession, at a dark depth,
Inheritor of his America maybe at its great height,

I praise him not in a loose form, not in outpouring,
Not in a positive acclamation of frenetic belief,
Not in the simplicity of a brotherhood, such peace,
And not in the dawn of an original compulsion,
But speak to him in the universe of birth and death.

By a Spring meadow I lay down by a river
And felt the wind play on my cheek. By the sunlight
On the water I felt the strangeness of the world.
Prone in the meadow by the side of the fast brook
I saw the trout shooting his shadow under the willow.

I sank into the mystical nature of memory
And became my beginning. I was one with strong nature,
At the heart of the world, with no need to penetrate her.
In the sheerness and the elegance of this feeling
I destroyed time and dwelled in eternal pleasure.

The vastness of the aim of human nature
Yielded to ease and immediacy of comprehension,
Such is the rarity of the mastery of existence
In the ethereal realm of pure intuition,
Within the subtlety of perfected spiritual balance.

160

II

What shall I say to Walt Whitman tonight?
Nothing that is not myself. Nothing for himself,
Who spoke the golden chords of a rough soul
Deep below the meeting of the mind
With reality; his words were a mask of the true soul.

I grew up among animal pleasures, hot in sense,
And fought off the lofty reaches of the intellect
As one knowing the soft touches of the night,
Running on the Spring freshets in delight,
Joyful and serene, not to be overcome or quelled.

Then dramatic evil like a blight overcame me,
The dream-like character of eternal knowledge
Was brought in earthly bondage; knowledge of death,
Our old enemy, appeared with his powerful will
And laid waste the garden of my green seeming.

The years began to whirl in a worldly ecstasy
Fulfilling some dark purpose confronting the heart
Of things, and I was loosened to flesh and mind,
Torn asunder from essential unity
And would wander the world in fateful duality.

This was the knowledge of good and evil,
This was the certainty of actual death,
The powerful hold of an ancient, fallen state,
The battering ram of time on the bones and eyes,
The new reality of the unredeemed mankind.

III

What shall I say to Walt Whitman tonight?
I look not upon the world of facts and figures
But in the heart of man. Ineradicable evil
Sits enthroned there, jealously guarding the place,
Only held at arm's length by a comic attitude.

Laughter at the sun and the moon, at the tides,
Laughter at the comedy of the etrnal struggle,
And at the institutions and society of mankind
Laughter, I celebrate this tonic attitude,
And go as far as that for the sake of intellect.

And run on bitterness and corrosive pessimism
Standing under the glaring eye of antique satire
And range the fields of powerful condemnation
As one who allows himself such pleasures,
A beast engaged, knowing the gates of escape.

New bombs, new wars, new hatreds, new insecurities!
Man has become the victim of delusions
Thrashing his brains in energies of misaction,
Lost in tribal sin, ready to destroy himself,
Defenceless against all natures of monstrosity.

What shall I say to Walt Whitman tonight?
Give us a share of your love, your simplicity,
The large scope, the strong health of the soul,
Love be our guide, and love be our redemption,
Love make miracle, animate us now.

IV

Love come upon us when the willow bends,
Love come upon us at the child's upturned face,
Love recapture us in the market-place,
In churches, slums, on mountains, in the fog,
Love be with us in the hour of death.

Love be with us in the pang of birth,
And throw out hatred, envy, pride, despair,
Be joyful at the time of the tall daffodil,
Be rampant as the legendary lion,
Be meek and sweet, and sure, so love be here.

Love that is swift creator and saviour
Bless all the infants and the old men,
Bless the middle kingdom of the workers,
Love come in the soft night, in the sensual day,
Let our airs be soft flower-lofts of love.

What would you say to me, Walt Whitman, today?
Is there anything you can give me but your love,
That total devotion to comprehension of the word?
It is not the forms you evoked, these are changed,
But the force you spoke with, the heart's holy rapture,

Your knowledge of the changeless in birth and death,
The merit of man in his eternal suffering,
Your love of the stars, of valour, and of doom
That I would say to you, Walt Whitman, tonight,
That you could say to me, Walt Whitman, today.

SOUL

I

The flow was toward the land,
It was a music of the altar deeps,
Impersonality of the proving waters.
Soul was coming to the landfall steeps.

The Soul was coming in it seemed at neap.
It made a faint halation in the air
As if a white, mist-fitted presence brooked
The high rocks with some supernatural stare,

Mysterious essence cleaving to the bushes,
That gave a strange elation, the good of man,
Subtle benediction like a waft of spume,
A sense, and then it seemed it was not there.

And came again before the mind had gone
Back seaward where the spirit was, that source,
And roamed a dream-like presence over earth
As if it had been always there, for man.

II

The Soul was fugitive, but it was fronds
Of palms from some soft South, palm-tones
Weaving the tides with rhythms warm and rich
That crept within the blood-dream like old time.

Then it was a presence of the memory
Walking on the land in heavy imagery
And gave so supernatural a sign
The heart rejoiced and had no more to fear.

The flow was massive as toward a midnight,
Sea-music deep as dreams of history,
And then it went away upon the air
Like silent boats pushed off the full-tide shore.

A holy feeling came upon the beach
And penetrated inward toward the woods,
Whether the Soul was far slipped out to sea,
Or whether a presence held the mind again.

III

Then it came upon the dappled waters
Across the farther islands, inward coming,
And seemed to be, in truth, the actual Self,
Safely stationed in the standing man

Who, breathing on the mystery of spirit,
Partook of insight, becoming a living Soul,
And was one with that going, and that coming,
The Self bound up within the eternal Soul.

Father of mankind, Soul that comes from deeps
And flows upon the land in fullest tides,
It is in mortal sonship that I stand,
With the heart's mystery in either hand,

And wait upon the judgment of the hours
That nothing should make clear this ancient praise
But ever keep, in mind alive and deep,
The dark intuitive presence of the Soul.

FABLES OF THE MOON

To keep an eye on fables of the moon
While feet are walking down the street
Is not the least a man can do,
And may be most.

I think of an old secret.
I walk upon the mart, and swear
It is a man's part so to do,
But not with my whole heart.

It is needed to be quick
And deal the world out with a will.
Gratuitous to think
On a sudden, summer whippoorwill.

SALEM

Madly she came, and stood upon the lintel,
With a look that you should never see.
And madly she handled the frail air,
Unimpeachable, a seer.

And with a visionary grace inwrought,
As who was moved by powers,
She was the representative
Of a teeming demonology.

On the hill there is a gallows
Still in the form of a blasted tree.
If you will look through the thinnest air
You will see what you will see.

THE RETURN

Still marvelling at the light,
Impersonal, on the mountain peaks, a halcyon
Glow; it strains to me,
To the last intimacy.

Then, quick to seize on intuition,
I thought I knew; now I know
I do not know. Time has refracted
Ineluctable meanings.

Now, the sight is more satisfactory.
Decades make us mountainous.
Life did not know what time could do.
My long light streams out to you.

THE GIANTESS

Idleness gilds an encompassing giantess
Who lies upon the heavy land of torpor.
Her yellow flesh, empty in indolence,
Poisons desire; she is mordant and depraved.

I have walked upon the golden stones of time
And fallen on her lurking on the hills.
My senses shrink within her slow, brutal languor.
She holds a sullen summer smile of lassitude.

She draws the spirit down upon the stones
And makes it as a gorged and sleeping snake,
Monster of disuse, elongate in her charms,
Where time is working its worn dreamlessness.

She moves in slowness of a long caress
And mauls the future. Languid and primeval,
She sucks evil away in one vast innocence,
And holds her victim mindless like a night.

Such hours of leaden torpor in her arms
Control an elemental misery;
While senseless of her flesh, her sensual power
Corrupts the longing and the love of death.

She is the mood of land-gone sailors when,
Their copra hoisted out at hot Copan,
They seek the thatch of love, and hope, but find
The girls are gone, never to return again.

THE WISDOM OF INSECURITY

The endless part of disintegration
Is that it will build again;

167

Of a robin,
That he will become a memory;

Of a hand-great August moth,
With eyes in his wings, so fine

As to represent himself as a fable,
That he will be tried again in a poem;

Of a petal-departed rose,
That it is its loving grandparents;

Of the evil of man to man,
That it is the tenacity of mankind

To put it out of mind in the long time
And commit to the heart new fidelities;

Of the broken music of silence,
That it will be brought together,

Renaming poetry; of the day's colours,
That they make the painter's paradigm;

Of immeasurable fallibility,
That it becomes art, by authority;

That the disintegration of time
Becomes the enrichment of timelessness,

So that nothing is destroyed, but finds
Its truth in the eternal mind;

That death provides nowise no escape.
Man becomes some other shape.

I must have come down from Adam
And am his metropolitan.

The leaves are falling and the rain.
Mystery is palpable. Sameness ever the same,

Ever different, where I look
Is through the fish to the fish-hook.

The strangeness of the poet's dream
Will set what is, not what seems.

When you see destruction itself
You see form out of the formless

As I recall in the Campo Santo, at Pisa,
The work of medieval Giovanni

Who painted an old man, prone and dead,
An infant, the soul, springing from his head.

SUNDAY IN OCTOBER

The farmer, in the pride of sea-won acres,
Showed me his honey mill, the honey-gate.
Late afternoon was hazy on the land,
The sun was a warm gauzy providence.

The honey mill, the honey-gate. And then,
Near by, the bees. They came in from the fields,
The sun behind them, from the fields and trees,
Like soft banners, waving from the sea.

He told me of their thousands, their ways,
Of pounds of honey in the homely apiaries.
The stores were almost full, in Autumn air,
Against the coming chill, and the long cold.

He was about ready to rob them now,
The combs. He'd leave them just enough to keep them.

I thought it a rather subtle point he made,
Wishing Providence would be as sure of us.

SUMMER LANDSCAPE

The pine with gray tips is moist still.
Peace pervades the scene. The standing pool
Has the green mantle, a spreading tone.
All the walks are full of time.

Vigour stirs the rose in thousand petals
As the fountains play; the frogs are placid.
It is a moist July. Rich the blood.
The snake will hold his poise, then glide away.

I have thought of pastoral simplicity
As flesh without a mind; it is luxury
Increasing summertime, as strokes of sleep
Accomplish better looks when birds are winging.

Swallows, for instance. There are swallows playing
About the barns like brightest minds; their eyes
Are quicker than my eyes; they make my mind
The quickness of their turning. I, their quick.

Cordwood stands beside the heavy vegetables.
Rank growths encroach in lower meadows; wild-
Run rough soil keeps a flaming need
Of growing trees, young pines forcing the landscape.

Everywhere is ease; everywhere is peace.
If an emotion comes, then put it back.
It is the stillest drama of stillness itself.
Poise is delicate, dedicating this instruction.

Now waves of the clover-ether triumph.
Space is a time of abundant silence.

The supple bees abound. The squirrels play.
The moonlight will be as good as the hot day.

ONLY IN THE DREAM

Only in the dream that is like sleep
When time has taken the measure of live things
By stark origination
Is mankind redeemed.

Only in the melancholy of the music
Of the midnight within the blood
Comes the fulfilment
After faring years.

Only in the balance of dark tenderness
When everything is seen in its purity
Do we penetrate
The myth of mankind.

Only in the mastery of love
Is anything known of the world,
Death put aside
With pure intent.

Only in the long wastes of loss
Comes the mystical touch on the brow
That triumph grow,
Insatiable, again.

NOTHING BUT CHANGE

We saw nothing but change in all the ways we went,
Nothing but time weaving wind, weaving the willows,
The tall buildings taken down and put up again
As we looked at them; the bridges made again.

We beheld the same of persons, nothing but change,
A kind of personal constancy we thought it to be.
Inured, we finally felt when somebody died
It was part of the flow of time, the nature of ourselves.

Then time itself began to get the upper hand
As our bodies, falling to the stress of air,
Left us to ridicule; Plato and Christ were bare.
A life-time of thought could not get through the flesh

And all the pledges of superlative intellect,
The rich, sensuous breasts of memory,
Fictions of the spirit, whips of the blood
Met denial, the unanswerable, God-given death;

The veritable and very rich death,
Without a poem, riches itself,
And when the gaudy play was enacted,
It was all a roundness, all a poetry.

THRUSH SONG AT DAWN

Bird song is flute song and a glory
Of the morning when the sun unascending
Holds his other glory of mentality

And the dawn has not the mental mockery
But the birds from sweet subconscious wells
Pierce through all barriers to sense,

They send and giving sing divinity,
So sweetly charged with subterranean meaning
They are like angels in the morning

Come from ancient time, a fast enchantment,
To bless our mortal songless weakness
And trail a vocal glory all the day.

172

I would not be a bird, but I would hear
Deep in some lost purity, beneath the mind,
There in the sweet, dark coil of time,

As in a mother, the thrush as saviour,
And a sovereign mediator; or any other
Lung-red singing: richness propounds confusion,

That pleasure that will never cease to be
Where we are played upon without a fault
By magic tones we love but do not have to know.

THE VOYAGE

To make a headway against the tide,
The tide-rip and the windy afternoon,
The skillful sailor, salt consigned,
Impressed the canvas to new subtlety.

The engine off, a sporting gesture.
Found him moving aft, heading fore.
Heading forward, we go backward
Where we were. The day is pure

And time seems stopped somewhere.
The sounding shore, we passed far back,
As ancient as Circean chant
And lure, comes to sound once more.

Now the consternated sailor winces,
His skill debased, the wind long gone.
The open ocean, a lolling torpid giant,
Occasions nothing but philosophy.

He turns the engine on again
As a last resort. Man cannot endure
To be going backward going forward.
The sirens wail in the rock's sonority.

OFF SPECTACLE ISLAND

Seals and porpoises present
A vivid bestiary
Delightful and odd against the mariner's chart.

The sea bells do not locate them,
Nor lights, nor the starred ledges;
We are unprotected from their lyricism.

They play in the blue bay, in day,
Or whoosh under the midnight moonlight;
We go from point to point where we are going.

I would rather see them playing,
I would rather hear them course
Than reach for Folly from Pride's Light.

THE SEASONS

Spring was never his fort. Suspect at first,
That is, at the first blush introspective, not first
When voluptuary to the inner arm, when durst
That smooth, round, and small quality, that nursed
Times earlier even to the earliest sensory charm,
As Burke would have it that way to be beautiful,
Not as the gowning roundness of the flesh growing,
Not absolute, that is it, and not a metaphor;
It was green, it was there, seen, hardly a
Thing seen, a deposition of some kind and style,
Overweening, but not a thing of criticism,
A lean-to in the gingery footstep forestation.

It was a trouble to the port. Whole scopes
Range in the vanguard of the watery ropes;
A voyage is many after-thoughts of hope.

Heroes have testy decks, not caulked in dope.
There is something lost in this misuse,
Minimal asphodels, worm-fat robins in the parks,
The structures of the erstwhile hyacinth,
And heavy gear of many a heady mallow,
No doubt. He cast his wits upon a sea
To find out. The nets trailed slime, green ooze,
And came out glistening in bright free gesture
Mounting, mounting time, genial Spring thrown out.

SPRING MAN

Summer was the problem of the universal,
The reductive mint-julep, seductive midnight recall;
The sweat upon the face; the glove homing the baseball;
Or the hand on the moonlit tiller, quiet as all;
No judicious panting after Heraclitus,
Nor fractions of Plato should burke the days' stale,
No frantic cry to Christ in the apt, higher stones,
Nor self nor soul lost or saved in mobbing thought.
Illumination. Without the need of intellection,
Imagination. Without the framework of doctrine,
Creation. Full as sense, time's melon, the scandal
Of elation. Love's game, matutinal, primeval.

The sun was the master of simplicities. The trees
Were a happy garden state, a golden grease.
He had the notion they could not decrease,
His flesh thus unguent and liquor, fat fleece.
The time of the year without fear, the pure time,
The time of the melon, and apple, the luscious pear
Still without a hint, burdening the fleshly air
Of anything but rich ease, heat weaving in air.
Not the mind, the flesh. All wholeness and wantonness
Was to human kind. The meadows with yellow sweetness
Would ever shine. Dance of the air-bees and blue brids,
The sea a brine of blood, ever without a mind.

THE MAN OF SUMMER

Autumn was the heavy mood of the human,
The heavy clutch of memory of everything known,
Lost and regained now in slow, gravid time:
He entered it as entering a world-mine.
He put his chances to this plunder. A long
Glare of introspection sealed the days in slow
Feeling, the half-closed eyes had seen too much,
And all was the sombre heaviness of betrayal.
Knowledge. The deep knowledge of the Autumn coming
To death's edge. The certainty of the decreasing future
Pledged imprisonment, that no backward look to tendrils,
Or vegetation, came without a harm or hurt.

It is the mind of the oldest Schopenhauer.
Recognition was within the hollows of the hour,
An inability to change, man without power
Empowered to see the truth; then not one flower
Would dance: not a thing would grow to fiction;
Not the salt sea dazzle in dalliance;
Not mountains inspire, nor metaphysic beckon.
The sufferings of man were every realization.
Autumn days! They hang upon the spirit like the flesh,
An exaggeration. Down to doom then man must go,
The old, the gay. See how the long centuries dwindle.
Do not stay. Knowledge is without power. O do not stay.

THE MAN OF AUTUMN

Winter is for Eskimos a castle of content,
Facetious in the furor of the snow; something blent,
Impure, high-pitched, finally an integument,
Destructive of the malice it engenders: embalmment.
It was what nature slyly left, but gets in full.
It is the mind's best, last chance and terminal,
The gaff of laughter, derision's joy, that icy joke
The deftest handle: satire of intelligence itself.

Zithers! Winter lacks the opulence to know.
It withers. It is the coldest, nicest predicament
Of dithery sheens. It is its own blight and refuse.
Whither? Winter is the purest intellectual dream.

It is significant on coldest winter nights
Love studies hottest: the animal has nothing quite
So straight an answer to that universal, white
And comic aspect of the natural blight.
And man will keep his courage, his provident esteem
Where most the elements stay mercury in spleen.
So in the deadness of the winter time
His blood, illogical, will seek the slime,
The melon, or even the withering of the vine.
Time play on. He cannot be dissuaded of his place
In the sun. Man is his own invention,
The Son of Man his timeless election.

THE NOBLE MAN

An Olympian before the Olympics, that inhuman backdrop,
The possible man, it is him I posit, him preempt,
The not incalculable master of the braced mountains.
He does not have to lose himself in them. His spirit
Creates their newest hazard as idyllic only.
He has confronted man, Olympian of the dark mark.

Rage is the substratum of pure animal poise;
A strenuosity, exquisite, roves in the controlled eye;
Multiple actions, muted, gaze upon the world;
Leaping tensions exhale the formidable and graceful;
Masterworking modulations enter every day;
Oval kingdoms quell the old volcanoes.

The Olympian looks at the Olympics profoundly,
In fervour. To him they are fractures of the Alpine.
Their height is modified in his height. Hurls
Fireballs out of himself when he wills it. Towers

177

Over his own music, lofty, sensitive, possessed.
The Olympian is master of his own mystery,

Mystified in his own mastery, recognizing
His relation to the real, the impersonal mountains.
He knows his own reality and that of the world,
The most human one, testator of furor and quiet,
He fears not, having feared all, loves altitude,
Gives off love's avalanche, mountainous man-make.

Fear that undoes many straightens him;
Contemplation is his burly action;
Round is the eye of his understanding;
Fear of death has not shaken him;
He looks upon all things with fervour of tenderness;
His laughter is ready. He has overcome pride.

An Olympian will not drown in the rain forests
Of self pity. Life gives him its own mountains.
Active love is the mark of a noble man,
By cynicism, by ascetiscism not betrayed. Nature
Works in him her balance. A bright perfection
Plays around the brows of the Olympian.

THE FORGOTTEN ROCK

Tawny in a pasture by the true sea
Ship-shaped it stood, the never realizable
Rock.

It was the awe placed on this natural object,
When looking at one thing, another world was seen,
He remembered.

Even this rock, sun-stroked, high-fashioned,
Peopling dream, enticing him completely,
Was never itself.

With such subtlety the blood, blue-watery source,
Leaped from one thing to something other.
A double escape,

A paragon of sight was posed upon
The blue rock; the excitation of the world
Glanced off.

This was nothing but the world itself;
A voyage in blue distance under tawny charges
Vividly known,

As a ship like a jewel of sense, come to
With boundless appetite, is yet unknown,
And is forgotten,

As we forget time that is thoroughly gone,
But was so certainly there. We annihilate time
To remember,

And what we remember is the duality of time.
The rock was never known as it was,
But as we are.

It had a cave with an obscure dome
A hawk flew into heading home,
Killed instantly.

ATTITUDES

IRISH CATHOLIC

After the long wake, when many were drunk,
Pat struggled out to the tracks, seething
Blinded, was struck by a train,
Died too. The funeral was for the mother and son.

The Catholic music soared to the high stones,
Hundreds swayed to the long, compulsive ritual.
As the mourners followed the caskets out
Wave followed wave of misery, of pure release.

NEW ENGLAND PROTESTANT

When Aunt Emily died, her husband would not look at her.
Uncle Peter, inarticulate in his cold intelligence,
Conceded few flowers, arranged the simplest service.
Only the intimate members of the family came.

Then the small procession went to the family grave.
No word was spoken but the parson's solemn few.
Silence, order, a prim dryness, not a tear.
We left the old man standing alone there.

AN OLD FASHIONED AMERICAN BUSINESS MAN

I asked no quarter and I gave none.
I fought it out until eighty-one.
Intelligence guided my efforts,
Cynicism dictated my business reports.

I played one off against another,
Keeping my head well above water.
I transmuted my blood to steel,
Early conquering the realm of feeling.

I taught ruthlessness by example
And hard work and steadfastness.
Now that the hated grave approaches
I wish for the love I could not give.

A YOUNG GREEK, KILLED IN THE WARS

They dug a trench, and threw him in a grave
Shallow as youth; and poured the wine out
Soaking the tunic and the dry Attic air.
They covered him lightly, and left him there.

When music comes upon the airs of Spring,
Faith fevers the blood; counter to harmony,
The mind makes its rugged testaments.
Melancholy moves, preservative and predatory.

The light is a container of treachery,
The light is the preserver of the Parthenon.
The light is lost from that young eye.
Hearing music, I speak, lest he should die.

PROTAGONISTS

To the man with his jaw shot away, blood-badged,
As he falls out of the sky to earth or sea,
Existence is lethal, and then it is not. Then

181

It is as it was in the beginning, and ever shall be.
  His mother sent him a Cross on Easter Day.

Last seen on Widener steps, holding a *summa cum laude*,
Otis Peabody, head large and capable as the stars,
Understood and understands the law.
A flak burst in the head destroyed the whole of Harvard.
  O you I admire—luck is a fatal absolute.

Here is a gay one home from the wars, Patrick O'Shaughnessy,
Keenness flashing from the Distinguished Flying Cross.
Of forty bombing missions over Europe, pilot.
He teases the room with a neat card trick, and
  Homer never had a hero half so grand.

But I see a man in blue denim walking, walking
Through the halls of conscientious objection,
Because he took Christ seriously, immured.
A literalist of the imagination! who
  Believed do unto others—Thou shall not kill!

A SOLDIER REJECTS HIS TIMES ADDRESSING HIS CONTEMPORARIES

Think no more of me
For I am gone
Where ages go,
No touch of snow
Nor sing-song bird sip song
Alters meadow.

You are whelmed in manyness
By days totally taken
By doing taken up

Summer and winter,
Plunger of fortune.

But I am hidden
And dropped out,
No more I count.
Flesh was fresh,
Time was evenness,
Death is stiffness.

Think only of the living,
It is the lips of wisdom;
Of wars perpetual;
Even of steadfastness
In man's misery.

'BLESSED ARE THE ANGELS IN HEAVEN'

Blessed are the angels in heaven
We are not with them on earth
And blessed is their rationality
Denied us from our birth

And if any can say
In our writhen, human condition
Proud, red words to make us gay
Let him say them and let him be

A man of courage in a broken time
And a great singer in the evening
The master of our irrationality
And lover of our writing

And the angels in heaven who are blessed
Will not hear him calling, calling
For they have nothing to do with us
And bind us to our barking heritage.

VILLANELLE

Christ is walking in your blood today,
His gentle tread you cannot hear nor see.
He tramples down your militant wish to slay.

The whelped deaths you dealt in your war's day
Arise howling, they will never make you free.
Christ is walking in your blood today.

You did it easily in the heat of the fray.
You did not know what you could do, could be.
He tramples down the massive wish to slay.

You are the front and fore of passion's play,
Of deepest knowledge you have lost the key.
Christ is walking in your blood today.

To kill is one, is not the essential way
Of action, which you then could not foresee.
He will wash the welling blood. Not slay.

A child becomes a man who learns to pray,
A child-like silence on a moveless sea.
Redeemed you may be of the will to slay.
Christ fermentative be all your blood today.

LIFE AS VISIONARY SPIRIT

Nothing like the freedom of vision,
To look from a hill to the sea,
Meditating one's bile and bible: free
From action, to be.

The best moment is when
Stillness holds the air motionless,

So that time can bless
  History, blood is a caress.

Neither in landwork nor in seawork
  Believe. Belief must be pure.
Let the soul softly idle,
  Beyond past, beyond future.

Let it be said, "A great effulgence
  Grows upon the sandspit rose.
A rare salt harrows the air.
  Your eyes show divine shows."

FORTUNE'S MIST

  The mists of fortune
  Blow with wayward cadence
  Within imagination
  Making chaos into sense.

  Man dreams his tribulations
  Strict and articulate,
  As Lincoln by a fire
  Wrote history on a slate.

  If not by absolutes,
  At least by artifice
  We cast our devils out
  To seek an angel's face.

  Strength in the hand and mind
  Holds to the central doom,
  Working reality
  In coping with a tomb.

  But for imagination's power
  Shaping the unseen

Fortune annihilates us
As if we had never been.

A heavy head of snow
Tumbling from a hedge
Is March's triumph; its revision
Is the poet's pledge.

Art gains in time
For it was deep in mind,
That rounded the waters,
And shaped the wind.

YONDER

I held Europe in my hand
Like a jewel that is implacable.
When I became most interior
I fled to my native land;

I returned to America, singing
Poets dead, long-living causes;
I loved them all. About them
I felt hypocoristical.

When the lovers walk on the Danube
And the thinkers vie in the park
I give my hand to the Big Horns,
I seek the Pacific in the dark.

AUTUMNAL

Action is a pain of being,
    Being is a rain of knowing,
        Knowing is a sense of self,
            Lovely the day

Thereof. Would you have it otherwise?
  A peak of ants of little size
    Obstructs me on the sidewalk,
      All clamoring talk.

The statues are lying around on the green
  Seeing what they have seen
    As lovers pass in the grasses,
      Elemental, massive.

Big clouds and little clouds cohere
  In arguments this time of year,
    Unclassified; they are lapses
      Floating, dappled.

Dogs are in and out. And bees
  Are falling into cider granneries
    Fat as unbuttoned fops.
      One drops, another drops.

We have been living the full year,
  It is still full, it is here
    In the late recline of sun,
      A red grand one.

What is going on beyond
  I have not found, am bound
    To the love of the unfound
      Beyond, but here.

THE SACRIFICE

Every poet is a sacrificial spirit,
Every song he sings is given
By special election in heaven
So that men may bear it.

Each toils, and throws his life away,
Gay as a boy tossing his cap up
For whether of tragic things and heavy
He lives in the senses' gaiety.

Like some drunken bee plundering flowers
Drunk with his gorgeous nature
He gives a golden summer afternoon
Its fiction, intellectual and sensual.

LUCUBRATION

Rain upon the window, rain upon the day.
The vastness of the stars ever upon us.
Fluid ripeness where the grasses totter,
A chill descending with another year.

Savageries of youthful indignation
Intimate the will: their lustful excellence
Flows out upon a red, eventual brightness,
All the future leads them up to dragonfalls.

O but the stealth and silence of the skies
And starlight far and starlight still and cold
Brings on the close communion with defeat,
The forceful draft of spirit's nightlong questioning.

And O again the children's vision, all delight,
That quick perfection seen as senseless innocence,
Against the rule of reason, regimens of solid day,
Perplexities of sensibility, the soul caught in a thicket.

Rain, the giving rain, leaves' quick departure,
The threading time, and blanketing, cold metaphor,
Time's dualism, where we heft the airy gait,
Where stares the negative stone, there Hynos waits,

Perhaps, some final, psychic resolution,
The tongue of fire upon the fuming water,
The eye of purpose in the lust of brightness,
Song's mastery upon the starlit tomb.

IN AFTER TIME

In after time, when all this dream
Becomes pure dream, and roughest years
Lie down among the tender grass,
And spring up sentient upon the meadow;

In that after time of great-born Aprils,
Beyond a century of tatters and of malice,
When love has thrown out fear and madness
The eyes will see the sun as wonder.

In after time, when rage and chaos
Lose their sovereign force, new dream
Will lift the shining life to spirit
And mate the make of man to merit.

Then shall holy summers come; then laughter
God-like shake upon a dewy morning;
Then fullness grow, big with purpose,
And man shall know again his richness.

A TESTAMENT

It is what I never quite understood
About my formidable day
Was the truth, the trust, and the good
Where the final values play.

It was the ungraspable part
As events and crises interfered

Was the bold quest of my art,
The blood, the crystal tear.

It was the lack of direct mating
With authority, politics or powers
Gave thrust to loving and hating,
Allowing the purest hours.

It is the world's inability
To nourish my senses whole
Brings on the subtle utility
Of the total strength of soul.

I sing of something so far and deep
Ages will find it clear,
Love that is a grasp, a leap,
And faith, landfall of fear.

Henceforth this testament
Of the struggles of my bone and time
Is made; for those meant
Who cast the spirit, seed the sublime.

REQUEST

For Dame Edith Sitwell

Will you write in a new book
Just your name,
In a new book, for me?

Will you write it plain,
In a new book, your name,
Just your name for me?

Will you make it an emblem
Of seventy years of joy,
Of pain, just plain, to see?

So that when I see this name
I see the turn of your hand,
The turn of the years I see

And think of the musical poems
That have made you swift and free,
The long waves of the sea

You caught in a life-time of
Rhythms to be, these
Caught in your hand to me.

Will you write in a new book
Just your name,
In a new book, for me?

LOVE AMONG THE RUINS

One time I was invited to see Croce.
Scylla and Charybdis lay between. In Sicily
The sky is blue over Taormina, flagrant
And dependable as a Greek statue.

The old columns were still taking the air.
It was a green, ethereal world, white Etna
Increasing the ponderable, inevitable nature
Of arcane spiritual adventure.

Over the sea Croce stared upon experience.
Insinuated within the discourse of events
A goddess appeared upon the stage declaiming.
She had ravishment, and sorcery, and authority.

Love was then the old debevilment
Of soul and sense; of fictions and mountains; of
Blue, green and of imperious whiteness.
Croce sat reading a book in Naples.

I swore to the gleaming gods of Hellas,
To the gloomy gods of America, and to these
Columnar shades above the turbulent waters
That I would search the white face of Etna.

I took my ease where the meanings meander
In crucial zones of mystery, where fire and ice
Commingle and life and death are one
And never went to see Croce in Italy.

ANIMA

We are betrayed by what is false. Within
Our hearts good and evil strive. Our minds,
Sometimes aloft, above grace, or sin,
Search out satisfaction. Time reminds

Our senses of the savage contradictions
Entertained tumultuously. We win,
We lose, we stay awhile upon convictions.
In some new century has any been?

The falsity is life itself. We are
Betrayed by time, which made us mortal. Time
Is a laughing light upon an ancient star.
Inmost thought is subtly made to rhyme.

It is the perdurable toughness of the soul
God and Nature make us want to keep;
The struggle of the part against the whole.
Each time we take a breath it must be deep.

THE SUPREME AUTHORITY OF THE IMAGINATION

Life longs to a perfection it never achieves.
Voices from the grave, with a wry grimace, whisper,
"We were never satisfied, we tried toward perfection,
We were undone. It is nothing to be a cipher."

Life breeds its joy in the incomplete.
A flag flying in a moment of the Atlantic
Lifts the spirit, lavishes a serene sign,
As halest happiness is death to the frantic.

Aesthetic purity stays with the rose bud.
Desire is renewed in every lover's glance,
The ununderstandable is always understood,
It is the shyest by the wall most wish to dance.

It is the grace to imagine the unimaginable
Elevates man to an angelic state
In which he may dwell, formidable and alone,
In the simplicity of the truly great.

It is the supreme authority of the imagination
Brings a frothed brightness to the human scene,
Bottle of industry, looking glossy-fine,
The blood-tip breezy and the anchor twined.

A rose of Spring seen with an even eye
Never betrayed the seer; he leaps the sight
And stands within ineluctable dominions,
Saved in some haven of a sheer delight.

PERCEPTION AS A GUIDED MISSILE

I

Resume unequal days, in chilly thrall
And in too hurting prisons; these four walls
For vistas plain; or those assumed through them,
My placid North, snow-bound in eyes as cold;
Upon my breast, with burn, the opposing South;
Cloy of ease, this East I nostril well;
And the windy gap, the damaging gray West.
But feet that feel are met by four plain walls.
His face! And all His grace habitual.

There is by snow a visible arrival.
I face this wall. Her face was dead, was clear.
Around, and by fire we are born intense,
Consume the essential gift desire, and feel.
I turn. Without giving or taking, lithely
Suspended, all timelessly is joy sweet.
I turn. And cringe at the brute savagery
Masterfully yelling, crazed by its own storm.
This; this; this; this; they seem the same,
Here prisoned where I count my steps all day,
In chilly thrall, and under the soft glare
Of the secret face of one adoration,
Attained; unattained; and unattainable
If walls were smashed, the sun plucked, and stars.

II

These distinctions chill me more. Proceeds
The unpleasant enterprise; heavy the footfall
That knows four ways, by rote, and those by walls.
Compelled; compelled. Inwaft, seductively,
The mellow rays of Eastern healing flowers
I fabric for a close worn cloth-of-gold,
So delicate, it is my skin's patine.
But the snake, that feeds on flowers, from my right side

194

Makes hiss with fatal passion, and in love
To the violent given force, I kiss, in joy,
In pain, the sting, annihilating the attraction.
Then, O terrible, the wolf ravenous
Rages ferocious, and I turn to the left,
Powerless, helpless, in repulsive fear
To be destroyed, swift fangs in the back.

Imprisoned. I seek the essential North with eyes.
Where flies around himself the albino crow.

The passage out will warm my brows apart.
The sun is of all these compact and stained.
Once held her spirit like a shape of sorrow;
The vibrant touch can give all death's load.

Often, most unsuspected, the dead face
Appears and brings; to make the present world.

III

I've been far off on seas, where compass light
Told North, South, East, and West, but night did not;
Nor blood, streaming in the wilderness
Of being, mute with ocean, and over-ocean.
All was roundness. The moveless turning ball
Allwhere, there; viewless, seen; and supreme.

Cold refusal. Pure walls of nothing,
Mortared well. Only the feet feel, walking.
Walls are often gates, and open vistas
Prisons. Each vexes with an angry stare.
I burn, to note the golden counterpart.
And tell myself aware by sudden feel.

You are surprised? But in no debt to cold.
I close my throat up with an humble pin.
And fret this brick-plot with an ardent heel.

IV

Along tender tangents, variant shocks contend;
Since between East and West a needle roams;
And not to the West entire must hearing turn;
And somewheres are to dwell, not delicate North.
Say away, say away these positive forming walls.
Bare intellection, willful absolutes?!
Too cold too long is betrayal too bare, too coy.
To fix an electric fluid in a square,
This terrible creative mirth and ring,
This piteous conditioned pain and cling,
This to-be-else, my tasted thwarting blood
Mortal. If they are, to see things as they are.
Ha, a man's just come in with an oilcan.

V

O lovely sun (like a singing boy),
With linger sweet, and marvel tone
Soft-coming too, be joy and woe.
And this my means: here on my given
Flesh, my flaxen bells of pleasure,
I play your warm resplendent shine.

VI

It is improbable, the faultless look.
Walls are harsh, and now my signs renew.
Scents; hisses; yells; and silences.
But love to one white adoration springs.
These doors, like tresses of a girl's dress,
Fling out, to let us deeper in, not out,
Where captive in the generous earth, a single
Spike runs from the sun to captive us;
And flaws freedom with the sweetest pierce.

VII

The way by thaw is looking-glass of sleet,
If senses can see, but mostly prospect sweet.
Smooth, warm, I think it ravishing since found.
The voyage is contorted by hot rain
And hail: only can spit-spit back in vain;
Yet noon's so sultry-lovely, time can beat.
No path is rescued betwixt hard stars of frost,
Where to fall foul, and there the world's lost,
On sharp cogs to you; the space between impounds.
At last your passage is extremed with ice;
It cracks, but snaps not its white device.
Endure, O mind, in circle that completes.

So smile; kiss; groan; all's on thin ice;
Save the volant crow, my master dear.
Save Him, who saves the world from sin.

BY THE STREAM

Every morning I wash the slate clean.
Each morning I sang, no such morning has been.
It is a springing, a green New England scene.

I wish to be deft in the stored morning air,
The past was locked in an immoderate lair.
Where there was stress, there would I dare.

By the living stream of language I
Threw down my lunch, dozing by an oak: try
As I could, I could not reduce the sky.

It was on a clear stream I teemed dreaming,
Prone and prevailing; I was that I seemed;
On my pied eyeball a blazing beamed.

On my noontime I, flushed and fashioned, fed.
To the earth, a gift of gloss, I gave my head.
From the stream I took the living dead,

The little newt, the yellow cowslip, water-shades
Loving their life in comprehensive glades,
I the many-bladed among the blades.

In this sweet, superior contention resting
My soul, a sailing bird on water, was nesting,
My green soul; it grew in the time's cresting,

When all of a sudden dark was coming on,
The basket empty, fragile, my musings gone,—
A glimpse of Love, and in the brake an unicorn.

WHAT GIVES

I shake an absolute around the world.
It is this: love never dies. It is alive.
This I tortured out in fifty years.

What others show, what I may know, before
Lung-blasting Death usurps my spiritual theme,
I do not know, but think will show the same.

As after years of rigorous spectacles
When evil mocked, and passion ruled and blazed,
And fear was lurking in a mullein eye,

There is the stealthy health of an hiatus,
Growth to a grandeur, strong and round.
Bring on blessings, Time, stay and sing.

Strength grows and throws around us holy love.
It is this I count on to the end of time.
Love is the end of knowledge, and sublime.

THE OAK

Some sway for long and then decline.
There are those, a very few,
Whose rings are golden, hard, and just,
Like a solid oak all through.

Each year builds on another truth,
A suffering, a joy increased in gold.
You cannot see, viewing the edifice,
Whether it is young or old.

Some have it in them to keep close
To nature, her mysterious part,
Seeming strange to be so natural,
Nature married to perfected art.

Flesh will ponder its dark blame.
Mind will never mate the true.
But the whole being will rejoice,
Like a solid oak all through.

IN THE GARDEN

Memory is a watery flower, when watered
Will transplant a scent from A to Z;
It is September. There are zephyrs truly.
A gold-banded bee in russet loam

Throws off the earth, his heavy cargo
At last aloft. You are the medium.
In you the subtle messages suspend
The alphabeta particles of gauze

Realization claiming permanence.
For these zephyrs, these sights and sounds,
That heavy bee, those indeterminate scents
Are not the world, but they are you.

You know them sitting in the shade
In old September, by the rich red banks.
The zephyrs are your mind, a probable
Stored world of melos appetite.

THE LOST CHILDREN

And so the river moves,
Impersonal and slow
Today. Let us go,
Afraid to own our loves,

To the place of ice and snow,
The brink where yesterday
Two children, held aglow,
Walked time away.

In a moment they were lost.
Ignorance and innocence
Pulled them under and tossed
Their souls up from sense.

Now, O stars, you hold
Their small souls, two
Children cold and old
In lissome Spring the true.

And so the river moves
Impersonal and slow.
We watch. Let us go,
And hold close our loves.

A COMMITMENT

I am committed
To the spirit that hovers over the graves.

All greatness flails.
Even evangelical Aristotle

Deploys his systems into mysticism,
Obfuscating his clarity of sight.

Plato goes with us on a picnic
As we mammock our hamburgers.

The logic of illogic,
The illogic of logic plays through time.

Poetic justice
Still is to get what we deserve.

I dream, here, now
Of the two-faced caprice of poetry,

Clarity of day,
Ambiguous necessities of night.

A spirit hovers
Over the stars, and in the heart.

Love is long
And art is good to stitch the time.

APPLE BUDS

Apple buds will never bloom
But to remind me of her room,
Impersonally proffering

Spring, when she was suffering.
She cannot take them in her hand
Again. I cannot understand
Her suffering, her suffering.
It is brutality to sing.

THROWING THE APPLE

(*Based on a painting by D. H. Lawrence*)

Adam and Eve sat in their garden.
The day was bright and fair, but Jehovah
Was looking over the garden as warden.
Would human softness ever harden?

Eve took a bite of the apple,
Concerned with the bright sun's dapple,
As shadows emerged in the woodland.
Adam's concern was to grasp, to grapple.

We then see Adam, unaccountably,
Stand up dark and fierce and shrill.
He aimed the apple at Jehovah
And flung it at him with all his will.

THE GARDEN GOD

Style is the water out of Homer,
    The way it flows. It never flows
        The same from the stone orifice
            Down into the garden pool.

Mark then that majestic head
    And fount of heavenly declension,
        The bubbles in the basin
            Making a merry noise and music.

Style is large and god-like, as if
  An elegance made life-like, and
    It seems to be an absolute,
      Curly locks, blind eyes, and sound.

Yet every day the water plays
  Differently from Homer's mouth.
    Each time I look thereon
      New enticement amazes me.

The winds of time will play the tune,
  A bird will come to sip alone,
    A cat will change the water-scene
      With arch and ritual concern.

I do not see our Homer plain.
  I see him melodious or restive,
    I feel the tensions of the day,
      The quick alarms, acclaims of change.

Style is magical despair
  Lest from the fount and source and power
    A single drop or grain
      Should lose itself from life's rich main

And it is plain for each to see
  In dream and consequence,
    The order of the oak and grass,
      The waving water's sound.

Or so I think replete
  With multitudinous harmonies
    On any day in summer here
      In the garden where our Homer is.

LIGHT FROM ABOVE

The vigor and majesty of the air,
Empurpled in October, in an afternoon

Of scudding clouds with sun breaking through,
Showing a militant light on mountain and river,

Is the imperial power
Greater than man's works

I praise and sing; my headlong delight
In unsymbolic gestures of eternity;

For here, surely, above the worn farms,
Their stoical souls and axe patience,

Whatever man learned from the soil, from
Society, and from his time-locked heart,

Is the greater, the grand, the impersonal gesture
And the imperial power; here, the great sky,

Full of profound adventure beyond man's losses,
Tosses the locks of a strong, abrasive radiance

From the beginning, and through the time of man,
And into the future beyond our love and wit,

And in the vigor and majesty of the air
I, empurpled, think on unity

Glimpsed in pure visual belief
When the sky expresses beyond our powers

The fiat of a great assurance.

AUSTERE POEM

Life in its brief episodes
Of sordor or of glory
Stains the flesh,
Baffles the intellect,
      Forces truth upon us.

Love in its vainglory,
Its deep commemorations,
Is at best a truce
Before subtle battles renew.
      Truth is forced upon us.

Hope renews egoism,
There are times of harmony,
Yet darkness obliterates light
And death overcomes life.
      Truth confounds us.

What is the best attitude
To take in incertitude?
What are pain and pleasure
But dazzled by enigma?
      May truth surround us.

Locked in mortal force
I speak in a locked estate.
I bend to my endeavour
And spend my love for you.
      May truth breed life.

HOOT OWLS

Owls that cry in the night,
(I have noted toward dawn)
Hooting in call and in answer,

Were supposed to be mysterious;
Indeed, their voice is enchanting,
With a far-away roll and fall,
Yet imagine my distrust
Of what used to be poetical
To learn that these dull birds,
Instead of leading us on
Into labyrinthian melancholy,
Actually make their hoots
To petrify, as it were,
And scare stiff small animals,
Who, thus mesmerized,
Cannot move for deadly fear,
Whereupon the hungry hoot owls
Wing down swiftly, killing
Their prey in handsome talons.

We must go elsewhere
Than the cry of the hoot owl,
Somewhere beyond realism,
For the tone of the poetical.

TREE SWALLOWS

One of the surprises of nature,
Sitting on an open porch
Overlooking oceanic summer waters,
Is the well-dressed, elegant
Tree swallow whose grace
Defies a sweep of pen
As he rounds a curve and,
Coming from out by the rocks,
From over the summer ocean
Drops down by your head,
Only an eye-shot above it,
Swiftly across to the tree
Ten sleek feet away,

Pulls up abruptly to it,
Places his feet on the rung,
And looks in, and goes in,
And then looks out adroitly
With a tailored, deft face,
Then steps out again
Eagerly, easily taking the air
In accomplished circuits
Catching gnats on the wing.

Especially toward evening
I watch his habitual flights,
Up high and aloft in air
Far out among the trees
Over the free coastline air,
Lost sometimes to sight,
But always coming back
High and swooping down,
Perfectly accoutred,
And as days go by in June
Every summer it is the same,
A svelte ritual of evening.
When he makes the nest
His mate will fly out and away,
And sometimes there seem
To be three, two males
And one female in the log-nest.
Elegance, grace and swiftness,
A well-tailored look, smoothness
And cheerful economy mark him;
As days and weeks pass
New duties come to the bird.

He takes his evening flight
As if in abandonment,
So easily, so splendidly
Swooping and turning and darting

But necessity is his
Like ours, it is purposeful,
He catches gnats on the wing,
Sometimes mouth-protruding bugs.
Now it is late in June.
He comes abruptly to the entry,
Just above my head and across,
I hear the little cries,
He stuffs each little throat
With a warm summer morsel
And off again, fair fatherhood,
To gather more for his family.
He seems carefree, seems eager
In airy freedom of motion,
Works around the apples and larches
And birches, up higher for mites
And returns, ever the elegant
Spirit of grace and duty.

In the heat of July
His capers increase, a pre-
Ordained change has come,
The parents go in and out freely,
The little ones peer quizzically
From the small round opening,
I dislike to see the days pass
Of such birdlinear charm,
But certainly as mid July
The last day will come,
Each day the same of each year,
The leave-taking. They are all flown.
And leave the mind to go
On its own accustomed flights
In its heavier manner
But bird-hearted all the same
For memory of leg-thrust
Up mountain rocks and leaps

Across chasms, and holding
The born clouds' lazy gauzes
As they twine off the peak,
And having an eye upward,
Being free, and coming home
To our own graces and duties.

THE CLAM DIGGERS
AND DIGGERS OF SEA WORMS

Appear far up the cove at low tide,
When the sea floor is a wet mastic,
Four men universal
In bent attitude of work,
Gray, mud-coloured, dun,
Caught in a moment of time
When a secret yield
Is possible to ancient earth—
I see them from a field
Under a cliff,
Almost static, scarcely moving
In their solemn grandeur,
The clam diggers,
The diggers of sea worms,
Placing their rakes down
Hard in the muck,
Loosening, pulling up,
Slowly manoeuvering,
Making rough black lines
In their slow progress
Disturbing the smooth, wet, black
Sea bottom of the cove
As sea animals may be
Making necessary tracks,
Solemn, ancient,
Then they became again
The living gray workers

Honest as surrounding cliffs,
Man making a living
From sea-fat residuums
When the sea has receded,
All gay boats and sails
Far off: earth-rich
Dark, gray men at work,
Impersonal as pines and sky,
I watch the heavy scene,
The slow, mute progress
Of torso, arm, leg and rake
As seeing a dark core
And sombre purpose of life,
Primitive simplicity,
Dignity beyond speech,
My mute salutation,
Time-deepened love
To clam diggers,
The diggers of sea worms.

A SHIP BURNING
AND A COMET ALL IN ONE DAY

When the tide was out
And the sea was quiet,
We hauled the boat to the edge,
On a fair day in August,
As who, all believing,
Would give decent burial
To the life of a used boat,
Not leave a corpse above ground.

And some, setting fires
On the old and broken deck,
Poured on the kerosene
With a stately quietude,
Measuring out departure,

And others brought libations
In red glasses to the sea's edge,
And all held one in hand.

Then the Captain arose
And poured spirit over the prow
And the sparks flew upward
And consigned her with fierce
Cry and fervent prayer
To immortal transubstantiation.
And the pure nature of air
Received her grace and charm.

And evening came on the sea
As the whole company
Sat upon the harsh rocks
Watching the tide come in
And take the last debris,
And when it became dark
A great comet appeared in the sky
With a star in its nether tail.

THE HARD STRUCTURE OF THE WORLD

Is made up of reservoirs,
Birds flying South, mailmen

Snow falling or rain falling,
Railmen, Howard Johnsons and airmen

Birds of Paradise
Silk lined caskets

Prize poems and guitars,
Beatitudes and bestiaries,

Children taught contemporary manners,
Time taking time away

With a haymaker or a sleigh,
Hope always belaboring despair.

Form is a jostle, a throstle,
Life a slice of sleight,

Indians are looking out from the
Cheekbones of Connecticut Yankees,

Poltergeists deploy northward
To tinderboxes in cupboards in Maine,

The last chock knocked, the vessel
Would not go down the Damariscotta

Until the sick captain's four-poster,
Moved to the window by four oldsters

Gave him a sight of her, and
He gave her a beautiful sign,

And there was the witch of Nobleboro
Who confounded the native farmers

Who, having lost the plow-bolt
Right at their feet, found it

Concealed in her apron: she laughed,
And made the earth fecund again.

The hard structure of the world,
The world structure of illusion.

From seeing too much of the world
We do not understand it.

There is something unknown in knowing.
Unfaith is what keeps faith going.

THE PARKER RIVER

(*To F.R.K.*)

I

It must have been a profound and a serene communion
When nearing dawn, still in pyjamas, to walk away
The body of this world, and give the body of yours
To the salt and running waters by the sea.

I gave my own son his first and baby dowse
In the Parker River: he cried with pain and joy together,
Knowing not that to go back to the sea
Is the great symbol of original mystery.

II

Is it right to take your life
Or better to let life take it?
Is it superiority of man
When things have come to such a pass
As his, the whole truth none else knowing,
To make a final affirmation
In a final, great negation?
Is it an intellectual grace
So to do, and, Oh far deeper,
Is it a spiritual unity
Known once and forever known
Between the doer and the Creator?

Or is it a cold, implacable knowledge
Of the lessening river in the blood,
A last defeat before a mask
Life always wears and never loses,

Inscrutable in its designs?
As who would say, I am the lost,
Forever lost, I am nothing now,
Of nothing, neither bad nor good,
My action is my final statement,
I too will be inscrutable
And none shall know my final meaning.
Mysterious action of a man

To walk into the river waters
Leaving wife, sons, time behind him,
The tidal river of the marshes
Sinuous and ancient, seaward
And landward ever moving,
As years move forward to our future
And backward to our past remembered,
Or caught in stillness at full tide
When time seems not, is not insistent,
And then the river seems a gauze
And we are perfect in its laces
Beyond action, within contemplation.

III

MOON

I incline and I decline,
I long toward mankind,
Oh in my passive glow
I all enchantment show,
Then, growing faithless-glimmed
To erring man who never
Loves me beyond my changes
And in his wild heart always ranges,
As if my own perfections were
Instead of brilliance, a dim blur,
I yearn back to father night
And pass mankind from my sight.

WIND

I try with every fret of feet
In measure like a dancer, neat
And true to every restlessness
And every hint of evanescence,
In my brunt and airy measure
I give with love my treasure
Rapt or easy, swift or slow,
Over field and meadow go
And come upon the human brow,
The shoulder, the sensing torso
To tell the secrets of the earth,
Coming from the realm of birth.

STARS

I am the spirit of the stars,
The all star, one welling impetus
August and final, beyond humanity,
Beyond wisdom, beyond finality.
And thus I am perfectly wordless
Serene beyond anything heard,
To whom the trials of mankind
Are like water running over sand,
So obvious and so mysterious
As to be beyond all seriousness
And in my timeless innocence
I contain all of experience.

NIGHT

But when weariness and harshness
Bring mankind into darkness,
When he pales upon the light,
Lost in the hives of sight,
When the strong are heartbroken
And in the lists of life no token,
Not one is worth the holding,

Such great mystery unfolding,
I am the dream of sweet peace
And the angel of an ease
Like water, like mother water flowing
Beyond the effort of man's knowing.

DAWN

And I am the dawn beyond life,
I come inevitably as the sea's return
In the small and happy estuary,
After the melancholy blankness,
With slow steps, and solemn renewal
Where the birds awaken to the true,
The most slow and certain beginning,
The inevitable, quiet winning,
I am the pure solution,
The forgiveness and the resolution,
The aspiration, the hope, the new breath,
I am the glory beyond death.

EARTH SPIRITS

We sing together our ancient song
Over man living short or long,
Beyond his breath, beyond his will,
It is strange kinship still
Whatever happens from his birth
In his pilgrimage on earth,
We too are mysteriously held
And mysteriously impelled
And in one nature we exist
And through one evidence persist
As river waters are bridal and coronal,
Baptism and eternal funeral.

Sons of his and progeny of mine
May swim again in the Parker River,
Loll in breast-deep fullness of the tide
Or let the current take them out, or inland.

There is a bridge near the swimming place
To go under, one way or another,
Alone or together, knowing or unknowing,
Loving the eternal flowing water.

AT THE CANOE CLUB

(*To Wallace Stevens*)

Just a short time ago I sat with him,
Our arms were big, the heat was on,
A glass in hand was worth all tradition.

Outside the summer porch the viable river
Defied the murmurations of guile-subtle
Truths, when arms were bare, when heat was on,

Perceptible as picture: no canoe was seen.
Such talk, and such fine summer ease,
Our heart-life against time's king backdrop,

Makes truth the best perplexity of all,
A jaunty tone, a task of banter, rills
In mind, an opulence agreed upon,

Just so the time, bare-armed and sultry,
Suspend its victims in illusion's colours,
And subtle rapture of a postponed power.

OSPREYS IN CRY

When I heard the call of the osprey,
The wild cries of the ospreys
Breasting the wind high above
The cliff, held static
On updraft over the ocean,
Piercing with ancient, piercing eyes
The far ocean deep

I felt a fleshed exultance
For the fierce, untamed beauty
Of these sea-birds, sea-hawks,
Wild creatures of the air,
Magnificent riders
Of the wind's crests, plummeters
Straight down for prey

Caught under water in talons
Triumphant as life,
The huge birds struggling up
Shaking heavy water off
And powerfully taking the air
With fish in talons head first;

I felt a staggering sense
Of the victor and of the doomed,
Of being one and the other,
Of being both at one time,
I was the seer
And I was revealed.

HALF-BENT MAN

Haunts me the lugubrious shape
Of a half-blind, burly, old
Man, half bent to earth

Who on the Princeton campus
Spears stray papers with a nail-
Ended stick, lurching, walking
Crankily, true scavenger
Ridding the earth of detail
And debris, always evident,
A bent man, the true condition,
Half-blind, but cleansing life,
Putting trash in a burlap bag,
He moves as it seems to me
With a profound, heavy purpose,
I am haunted by his life
As towers, books, professors, ideas
Mingle in a world beyond him,
But it is his own, dark burdens
In his bent, half-seeing, weary attitude
I claim as man's and mine,
And O blind-man, rag-picker,
Paper-picker, cleanser of domains,
I shall not betray your meaning
As time bends us to the earth
And we pick what gems and scraps
There are from magnificence.

SPRING MOUNTAIN CLIMB

Till thinking had worn out my enterprise,
I felt, and felt the flesh
Salt-swart, blood-sweet,
To which bird-song stung mysterious
And the white trillium mysterious in the wood;

I saw the mountain and the lake,
I followed where the source sounded,
Over boulders, crossed logs,
Up rugged reaches, where
The gates of mystery increased;

Sacred justice moved me, I entered
The ancient halls of visionary grace,
Bird-call sounded, sky
Appeared miraculous along,
And evil thickets held red histories;

Here divine justice made me sweat;
While an eye nebulous and profound
Partook of a huge nature, endless
Sufferings redeemed in rushwater,
Song falling, searching the world.

Such were the signatures I saw
Written by the hand of God
In knotted density, mysteries
Of incontestable day, while I
Passed the singing brook, so

Controlled by its eternal sound
As to be a living witness
To spirit, and to spirit reaching,
And to the sound falling back,
And man fallen to his endless burden.

THE PASSAGE

Disindividuating Chaos
And old Discord clamped

Down on my downy love
Before it was spoken of,

Suckled must be in a year
First fingered; sensed no fear,

Then shot up in the blue sky
Conclamant with ability,

O I remember the holy day
When glory along me lay

In brightest shoots, singing sunbursts
And honey-great thirsts.

Then power came with outer throng
And dense strife of tongue.

II

With power came delight
Which put the world to right

Before ever it was wrong,
Incredible joy, poem-song.

Early then I knew
It was a gift of the true,

I struck a dangerous course,
Reckless a spendthrift. Source

Was sure, great world-brightness
Washed clean in lightness

Opened along my ego,
I danced alone. I would go free

With a will never tame
In the soul's single aim.

III

I took the world alive,
Drew honey from the hive.

Experienced quickened,
Then discourse thickened,

The heaviness of a fall
Fell like a blight over all,

I jostled in sea-spate
Of world-wrestle, dared fate

To tell me the worst
And fell on pain, and cursed

The doom upon the race,
The death in every face,

And when I saw men die
I heard their holy cry.

IV

Dense was word-drift,
Nor could the senses lift

To purity of Psyche dream
But dream would deeper seem

With knowledge in every breath
Of loss, suffering, death.

I came into dark hours
In the loss of powers

And wove my life with men's
Detentive stratagems.

I spoke beyond the nation
In imagination

And loved the mortal mind
Of timed humankind.

V

Language became
The unifying aim

In density and purity
Of all we can see,

The statements of the eye
Gained strong clarity,

The reaches of desire
Became a holy fire,

Words of fire to fashion
The song of man's passion

And over the brooding hurl
Of world's meaning, a furl

Of peace and ease, sight
Of unity, the holy light.

VI

But ambivalence and terror
Struck everywhere in error

And in errors of living
My world-force was giving

Compulsions of the blood
In pluralistic love

As effort steepened,
As years deepened,

Darkened to satiety
By a palled society

Within materialism,
Without aerialism

Of the soul's light
And joyful fight.

VII

Beside a river I stood
Nearby in a wood

Where was a spring
And in it a thing

That looked like a cup.
I wanted to lift it up.

It was hidden in mould,
Looked broken and old.

I bent, and reached down
To an invisible town

Where antique lovers danced,
In bright air entranced,

And came to grips,
And put it to my lips.

THE GODS OF WASHINGTON, D.C.

I was wondering about the gods
As I was walking down Constitution Avenue
For always since I was a boy
I was conscious of the gods in the offing,

Always off there somewhere in the air,
Never immediate and satisfactory,
Yet indubitably the master stuff
And living and seeing of our being,

And now here on Constitution Avenue,
With memorial buildings austere and white,
I wondered about the gods of the world,
Their existence, their glory, and their authority.

The gods were so plural and so vague,
Yet so powerful and so composite
That I was perplexed on Constitution Avenue
Even as I had been perplexed as a boy

And nurture this poem about the gods,
Who spring and leap out of our blood,
As one still seeking for definition
At odds with, but admitting the gods

And if they were a fallacy or illusion
May they go back before their birth,
But if they are a waking fact and a conclusion
May they state their case and return

For in this century of delicate balance
We have need of the gods of the air,
Stout gods, stubborn as bony man,
But we ought to know whether they are there.

EQUIVALENCE OF GNATS AND MICE

As a pillar of gnats, moving up and down
In June air, toward opulent sunset,
Weaving themselves in and out, up and down,

As diaphanous as visual belief,
In scintillant imagination, is slightest dancing,
Weaves a major harmony of nature;

As tiny field mice are saved from the sickle
By a lean seventy-year-old scyther in Maine
Who brings them in, saying, "They have enemies enough";

Who are hand-fed by a dropper on milk and water,
Hoping the small creatures will survive and thrive,
Slight event against the history of justice,

It is necessary to hail delicacy
Whenever encountered in nature or man;
No disharmony come near this poem.

BIRTH AND DEATH

I dropped to depth,
And then I leaped to height,
But in between was the fearsome place.

All imaginative skill
Could not shape the in between,
While depth and height were absolute.

I called in philosophy,
With mortarboard on top, to help;
The serious gambit of wisdom.

And I called on love,
Great bounce, good thrall,
Knowing the happiness of lovers.

And action called on me,
Saying, take the sea, the sky;
Yours is the enthusiasm.

It was like the drama
Of a man thinking he
Could outwit life itself,

Like the search for purity,
Irrational struggle of the will,
A might and power and force.

The in between will not be conquered
So long as man shall strive
And struggle with the world.

I dropped to depth,
And then I leaped to height,
But in between was the fearsome place.

THE INCOMPARABLE LIGHT

The light beyond compare is the light I saw.
I saw it on the mountain tops, the light
Beyond compare. I saw it in childhood too.
I glimpsed it in the turbulence of growing up.
I saw it in the meshes of meaning of women.
I saw it in political action, and I saw
The light beyond compare in sundry deaths.

Elusive element, final mystery,
The light beyond compare has been my visitant,

Some sort of angel sometimes at my shoulder,
A beckoning guide, elusive nevertheless,
Under the mind where currents of being are running,
It is this strange light I come back to,
Agent of truth, protean, a radical of time.

The light beyond compare is my meaning,
It is the secret source of my beginning,
Issuance of uniqueness, signal upon suffering,
It is the wordless bond of all endings,
It is the subtle flash that tells our song,
Inescapable brotherhood of the living,
Our mystery of time, the only hopeful light.